The Sugar Daddy Formula

A Sugar Baby's Ultimate Guide to
Finding a Wealthy Sugar Daddy

BY

Taylor B. Jones

Published by:
R&D Publishing
12460 Crabapple Rd Suite 202-128
Alpharetta, GA 30004

www.theSugarDaddyFormula.com
Email: press@sugardaddyformula.com
Phone: 877-784-9302

Page and layout design by Perseus Design

Print ISBN 13: 978-0-6157650-9-9
Print ISBN-10: 0615765092
E-book ISBN-13: 978-0-9893273-5-0
E-book ISBN-10: 0989327353

Contents

About the Author

Taylor B. Jones, Lifestyle Coach for Sugar Babies, creator of The SugarDaddyFormula.com, and author of *How To Ask Your Sugar Daddy For What You Want...And Get It*, has provided thousands of Sugar Babies just like you with the tools and resources they need to achieve the ultimate Sugar Baby lifestyle they desire. With a passion for human behavior and for discovering the nuances of personalities types, Taylor has become a master of how these attributes can be used by a savvy Sugar Baby to influence Sugar Daddy behavior. Her Sugar Daddy Formula will change everything you know about being a Sugar Baby. The most recent in her series of sensational eBooks, *The Sugar Daddy Formula* provides you with the opportunity to discover the secret for finding your perfect Sugar Daddy.

Foreword
by Leidra Lawson

Taylor B. Jones' book *The Sugar Daddy Formula* is a must-read for modern Sugar Babies wanting success in finding a Sugar Daddy. When she doles out her practical advice, Taylor is a cross between "big sister meets Sugar Daddy dating expert." Chock full of great tips for serious minded Sugar Babies, whether experienced or new, Taylor's book can help any Sugar Baby avoid the pitfalls of Sugar Daddy dating. The book is written in a straightforward way with easy to follow steps on every page. It's obvious she cares about teaching women how to be great Sugar Babies. The steps outlined on profile writing have a good dose of business savvy with marketing techniques that an MBA would use in doing a new product launch – and this is exactly what Sugar Babies need in order to compete in the Sugar Daddy dating landscape.

All you Sugar Babies out there, read *The Sugar Daddy Formula* and get ready to meet the Sugar Daddy of your dreams!

Leidra Lawson
Author of *Sugar Daddy 101*

Preface

I didn't want to write this book. In fact, it's something I thought I'd never do. In many ways I was as embarrassed to write this as you may be to pick it up. And that's fine. It means we're in this together.

Let me tell you why I'm embarrassed. Then I'll tell you why you're embarrassed. And then we'll agree to move on and to recognize that we're here on the same page for a reason.

It's easy to look at someone as they are now and see all they have achieved. But that same person started like everyone else. I have good days and bad days. I struggle with how I view myself and the color of my skin. I'm not a blue eye bombshell. I'm not a model. I'm not a celebrity or reality star. I wouldn't call myself a Sugar Baby. I am a woman who has chosen to enhance my life through my relationships. It's what everyone labels me and my relationships that they don't understand. I embrace it. Labels make us feel better. It makes us sleep better when things are in its place and helps us make sense of this life.

I know how hard it is wanting to be in a better situation than where you are right now, and having no help or the financial resources you need because I struggled myself. Therefore I now use what I learned to deliver information into the hands of Sugar Babies, giving them the "how to's" by increasing their success rate with Sugar Daddies to get them what they want, and a better life.

I wish I could remember when it all began.

In fact, I was a tomboy growing up (insecure about my looks) and my first business was run out of my bedroom.

My family was not entrepreneurial. My friends were content with dealing with men who walked all over them and took advantage of them. I didn't know a thing about Sugar Daddy dating let alone knew that I was a Sugar Baby. I didn't have Sugar Daddies providing me an allowance because I joined a dating site and labeled myself a Sugar Baby. AND I didn't have any venture capitalists funding my ideas and sprinkling my businesses with magical sugar dust.

But I had the one thing that made all of the difference: Motivation.

I never set out to become a Lifestyle Coach for Sugar Babies.

But I started at the beginning just like everyone else. Like you, I've always been attracted to worldly older men, and I wanted to surround myself with them to get inside their heads and experience a different lifestyle than what I was accustomed to. Perhaps it was the maturity and the wisdom they provided and the guidance I yearned for.

It changed my outlook on relationships, regardless of how old or young the partner is. When you have a relationship, you have to get your wants and needs from that person - and if you're not getting it in your existing relationship, you will seek it out until your needs are being met.

Then I had a reality-shattering experience — one of those moments that altered the course of my life. I discovered on the Internet a place where women just like you and me enjoyed access to wealthy suitors.

I disguised my identity and knocked on the door of that world, and it slowly opened. Once inside, I thought my own frustrations, fears, and personal dilemmas would be released. I became obsessed with wanting to know more about this world. I came across books about being a Sugar Baby, but they only left me wondering what to do next. How could I actually make their stories my own? I had no one to ask or turn to for help. I was alone.

The other women didn't have those keys I was looking for. But I wouldn't trade the journey I took for anything. It taught me something I never would have realized on my own: that with my passion for human behavior and for discovering the nuances that drive a man to give a woman what she wants, I could create the system that has worked for me and which I now share with you.

Even though I had no intention to create the Sugar Daddy Formula, I set out to offer a place where Sugar Babies could connect and not judge each other, and where we could help each other with the personal issues that we encountered. I started doing a few things in my spare time to help the many women who reached out to me with emails, calls, and letters full of stories. A few turned into hundreds and then turned into thousands. And most of these women were not escorts or gold-diggers, but women just like you and me who were looking to enhance themselves.

So I decided to take my heels off. You're now wearing those heels. But this book is not just a story, at least not in the proper sense of the word. It's a how-to-book. The story is not mine to write but yours to live. The pages will be turned by your own motivation.

I consider myself to be a chic entrepreneur and a Sugar Baby. I teach Sugar Babies with the "know how" to get what they want from their Sugar Daddies - and I teach them how to do it with proven, guaranteed and easy-to-follow steps that accelerate Sugar Baby success.

The Sugar Daddy Formula is the guide on how to get what you want out of your relationships. I'm proud to share my experiences and advice with you, and I hope that you'll join the conversation.

I've spent the last several years personally testing all of the different strategies that everyone else just writes blog posts about.

I will show you. I give advice from a place of experience. I'm not concerned with being right. I'm only concerned that you find your ideal relationship and the lifestyle you desire.

You don't have to be in control of your Sugar Daddy dating to be in control of your Sugar Baby lifestyle.

Once you make that first step and instead of waiting for a site to put you in reach of a Sugar Daddy, you TAKE control — everything can change.

Do you know what you are selling as a Sugar Baby?

Everybody is selling something.

It is the most difficult thing in the world to make a human being do anything.

You can make a dog jump through a hoop. You can even make a mule do what you want him to do if you're persistent enough.

With people it's different.

The surest way to antagonize a Sugar Daddy is to give him the idea that you are trying to force him to do something.

When a Sugar Baby says to her potential Sugar Daddy, "You must provide me an allowance," he has a tendency to refuse.

And let's say that your potential Sugar Daddy can provide you with what you want. Why doesn't he?

Simply put: **He can't afford you mentally.** Reread that.

That means: He doesn't feel he can get enough value out of your relationship to justify investing in it.

It comes down to price elasticity. Everything has a price. Everyone has a price (standard.)

And with that comes price resistance.

So you have to do one of two things:

- Lower the price, or come up with a packaging he can't refuse to let you pass him by.

- Your price (worth) depends on the value to your potential.

It all boils down to how well you can sell yourself.

Do you know what you are selling?

You are in the business of selling yourself.

- You see, it doesn't matter what situation you are in.

- It doesn't matter how old you are.

- It doesn't matter if you are a supermodel or not.

You are selling yourself.

How you present yourself is based on how well you can market yourself.

Marketing is marketing. And marketing is always going to be marketing.

All techniques of selling yourself to Sugar Daddies are evolved from this basic rule – make Sugar Daddies want to do things for you.

We're all motivated by the same basic pleasures and philosophies.

Sugar Daddies are still men. Men have emotional triggers.

Which is why, you've got to know and understand Sugar Daddies, understand what stage of the game you are in and making sure you are getting the right Sugar Baby marketing messages to your ideal Sugar Daddy, and developing the right approach.

So, bottom line:

- Who you are doesn't matter.

- Your age doesn't matter.

- Your race doesn't matter.

Marketing is marketing is marketing.

If no one teaches this lifestyle to you. How are you supposed to know? I will.

By being here; I am sure you feel the same way.

First, let me make a few things clear.

The number of Sugar Daddies you attract is directly related to...

1. Your ability to market yourself effectively to your ideal Sugar Daddy.

2. Your ability to convey your perception of your wroth to your target to get what you want.

3. Your ability to get the cooperation of your Sugar Daddy to want to provide you with what you want.

Now, I want you to notice that nowhere did I say "You need to be the next Top Super Model."

I also didn't mention anything about "race" and "age."

"Why?" you ask.

Because none of that matters.

It's about how well you can sell yourself to your target, and making the right connection.

Now it's UP TO YOU to take action. Because knowledge is meaningless without action.

Introduction

When you say the words "Sugar Baby," there's often a look of disgust that comes across someone's face. Immediately they think "escort" or "gold-digger." It's not something you tell your parents or friends, and you immediately feel as though you're alone in this journey. You haven't got a map and you must find your way by trial and error.

Many of us keep our Sugar Daddy dating a "dirty little secret" and we never talk with anyone else about it...so we're left to wonder if we're the only one dealing with the issues we're going through. If you have ever wondered this, the answer is, "No! You're not alone!"

As women, we all have the power to attract and the ability to draw Sugar Daddies in and hold them in our grasp. Far from all of us, though, are aware of our potential, and we imagine this lifestyle to be a mystery that a select few will ever experience. Yet all we need to do to achieve our potential is to understand what is in a person's character that naturally excites them, and develop these qualities within us.

Successful Sugar Babies are rarely supermodels. That's a misconception. Being a successful Sugar Baby begins with your character and your ability to radiate some quality that attracts Sugar Daddies and stirs their emotions in a way that they want to help you.

Most of us understand that certain actions on our part will have a pleasing effect on the potential Sugar Daddy. The problem is that we're generally too self-absorbed: We think more about what we want from this lifestyle than what *they* need from us. We may occasionally do something that interests the potential Sugar Daddy, but often we follow this up with an aggressive demand because we're in a hurry to get what we want. Or, unaware of what we're doing, is showing a side of ourselves that comes across as petty and deflates any illusion or fantasies a Sugar Daddy might have about us.

You will not get what you are looking for out of this lifestyle by simply labeling yourself a Sugar Baby or merely joining a Sugar Daddy dating site. Attracting a Sugar Daddy is a process. It's an art that requires patience, focus, and strategic thinking. You need to always be one step ahead of your target.

The Sugar Daddy Formula: A Sugar Baby's Ultimate Guide to Finding a Wealthy Sugar Daddy will arm you with a series of powerful tactics that will help you find your

Sugar Daddy and live the lifestyle you want. I'll reveal the secrets to making a dating website profile that will captivate the Sugar Daddy that you want, including tips on how to craft your message and post your photo. You'll learn how to tell if your prospective Sugar Daddy is a poseur or the real thing, and how to take the relationship beyond the first date. We'll discuss when to have sex, and when you need to talk to him about your allowance. *The Sugar Daddy Formula* breaks down the different types of Sugar Daddies and what you can expect from each one – and what they expect from you! And to top it all off, I present real-life case studies that you can learn from, plus additional resources.

There's so much more – but I'm dying to get started! I know you are too – so let's get our journey underway and find you the Sugar Daddy you deserve!

Part One:
The Essence of Sugar

1 Questions and Answers

First of all, let's start by asking and answering some of your most basic questions. Don't be shy: we're going to speak frankly and as friends. If you want, go and grab a cup of coffee. I'll wait.

Ready? Okay, here we go!

What is a Sugar Baby? An SB (as we'll call her) is a woman who aspires to associate with a person or persons (usually a man, but could be a woman, too) who have proven in their lifetime that they have accomplished more than just the status quo, and have achieved a certain status in life that affords them an advanced lifestyle. A Sugar Baby is a woman who desires to enrich her own lifestyle

1

by associating with men who have proven that they appreciate the rewards that dedication to the achievement of certain standards affords them. Such a man is a Sugar Daddy (SD). By associating herself with such men, a Sugar Baby aspires to enrich her own status in life and will also enjoy the enriched benefits such a lifestyle can bring. Achievement can take on many forms, but the common denominator in the SD lifestyle is the innate desire for emotional and material enrichment.

What does a Sugar Baby provide? The role of a SB can take on a very complex set of parameters. By their very nature Sugar Daddies tend to be exacting and driven individuals who strive for a certain complex threshold of perfection that is normally not achieved by the average individual. Consequently, the role of an SB can take on many forms and is usually always a dynamic variable in the relationship. An SB who understands her role must often wear the hat of a psychologist, a nurturer, a confidant, sounding board, and above all else be a true understanding partner to the inherent needs of her Sugar Daddy. She must understand that each SD is unique with unique needs and approaches. An SB should at all times be searching for ways to provide emotional stability for her SD while at the same time trying to enrich her own station in life. Often times this can become a sensitive balancing act between her own needs and desires and those of her SD, but at all times the Sugar Baby needs to keep in mind that her chosen SD is the vehicle that will provide her with the goals and aspirations that she truly seeks in enriching her life.

What is a Sugar Daddy? An SD is a man who aspires to an advanced level of achievement and excellence in his professional life, and who will never compromise that same desire in his personal life. It's that simple — and once aspiring SBs learn that if they truly want the benefits of this lifestyle they must accept the fact that they're dealing with very driven individuals who strive for something far beyond the average.

What does a Sugar Daddy contribute? An SD who has learned to care for his SB can provide many emotional and financial assets, both in the short term and the long run. If a Sugar Baby takes the time to learn what lies beneath the outward shell of her SD, she can tap into an untold fountain of resources that most never dream of achieving. The very nature of the SD and his achievements would suggest that he has separated himself from the mediocrity of the masses, and consequently has the resources and experience necessary to enrich the woman he chooses to contribute his time, money, and efforts towards. If nurtured and respected, the Sugar Daddy will return the investment in emotional energy many times over, and there are few boundaries or limitations as to what an SB can realize. An SD who has chosen to allocate his emotional investment in a deserving SB can literally be the conduit to life's enrichments.

What's society's chief misconception of the Sugar Baby and Sugar Daddy? The typical misconception is that an SB/SD relationship consists of an avaricious woman willing to perform any duties or sexual acts for an affluent man in return for money. Of course it can happen, but when the relationship is only about sex it exits the realm of a true SD/SB relationship and becomes that of an escort or call girl and her John. A true SD/SB relationship is conducted between two individuals of discerning tastes and ambitions in an effort to provide the other with the enhancements of an affluent lifestyle. Often times this relationship is misunderstood by those whose only objective is to extract money or financial benefit utilizing sexual favors in return. The true SD/SB relationship could not be farther from this reality.

What can people learn from the relationships of Sugar Babies and Sugar Daddies? If individuals will take the time to truly analyze and study the true essence of an SD/SB relationship they will quickly come to the realization that such an association actually is developed on a mutual foundation of trust and respect between two individuals who have defined their goals and aspirations in life and have developed a true purpose for their existence. The most beautiful relationships in life are those that are forged between two individuals who have defined their expectations and are attempting to enable each other to achieve those dreams.

What should all Sugar Babies know if they want to pursue this lifestyle? Every SB should realize from the outset of her journey that her SD is an individual with intrinsic emotions, wants, desires, and human frailties just as any other individual. In many cases, because of the intensity of those emotions framed in an overachiever, he's many times more pronounced than the normal individual. She should take the time to carefully analyze those personality traits in her SD and make every effort to attempt to enhance his mental well-being by nurturing and truly caring about the events that on a daily basis are affecting his life.

To sum up in one phrase what a Sugar Baby should endeavor to adopt as her relationship goal, it is this: she should always strive to "Life Enhance."

2 Get Ready for a Dose of Honesty

I read a lot of Sugar Baby Blogs and follow a lot of Sugar Daddy dating site blogs, and let me tell you: Sugar Daddy / Sugar Baby advice is the worst.

Here's a typical example. "Sally" was asking for advice about a potential Sugar Daddy she was seeing. They had gone on a few dates. Yep, she had sex with him. And guess what? He rarely called her and when she initiated contact he mostly sent short text replies. He had yet to provide her with anything that she looking for in the relationship. (If you could call it a "relationship." I'd call it a one-way ticket to Loserville.) The advice she got from the blog forum was typical.

"LEAVE HIM!" the other women on the forum yelled.

"Here is what you do," one said. "You need to be blunt and ask him for what you want."

Another said, "Let him chase you. You need to filter out Sugar Daddies like this and go for men who want you."

But do you notice something funny about the advice?

Not one person told Sally to improve herself.

Instead, they told her about filtering Sugar Daddies... and how he needed to work to win her... and how she shouldn't put up with the way he was treating her.

Yes, Sally should probably kick that guy to the curb because he's getting his rocks off without providing her with a mutually beneficial relationship. But I guarantee you that Sally could, and should, improve herself.

This idea of actually improving yourself is advice nobody tells their friends. It's politically incorrect and impolite, and it's easier to tell them to dump that loser! But it also happens to be 100% true. I want to show you what I mean.

A friend of mine, Roseanne, had a crush on a big-name, top-tier guy. She was mystified that he didn't seem to be into her, and she asked for my advice.

I said one thing: "What kind of woman does a man like him want?"

Roseanne responded with generic BS answer: "Confident, smart, blah, blah, blah."

I said, "Ok, just stop. This is a high-caliber man. He is swimming in women. Of course he wants that — but that's just the price of admission. What else?"

She was stumped, and admitted she'd never really thought of what he would want — because in her mind, for her entire life, she'd been the prize that men pursued.

It turned out there were a few things she could work on. She recognized that to attract a top-tier partner, she had to be at the top of her game.

I'm telling you this because I'm not here to make you feel bubbly-y good; I'm here to help you improve and live the lifestyle you want. And sometimes that takes brutal honesty.

We do the same thing when we're on these Sugar Daddy dating sites. We write about what we want in a Sugar Daddy…how we want to be pampered, be provided with shopping sprees galore, and how we need to be compensated for allowing a man to breathe the same air that we do.

I call this the "I, I, I Syndrome." Wannabe Sugar Babies spend so much time thinking about what they want that they fail to pay attention to what their potential Sugar Daddy wants!

Pay close attention here: If you're on these dating sites, go ahead – create your profile, post a picture, and wait.

You can wait around for weeks and months, and I'll bet the only result you'll receive is dead silence. You'll be puzzled by what is happening because these dating sites paint the image that you will find a Sugar Daddy instantly.

Or, you can deeply understand your potential Sugar Daddy and shortcut everyone else.

The fact is that eighty percent of your work is done *before* you ever start being in a Sugar Daddy relationship. Wannabe Sugar Babies want the magic bullets — "Taylor, what should I say when setting up a relationship to ask for what I want? What's the magic phrase?" The truth is, eighty percent of the work happens before you ever get what you ask for.

If you don't understand the psychology of barriers, no amount of fancy scripts will help. This is why newbie Sugar Babies always want to know, "What do you say to him? Tell me!" but they fail to understand that no script will persuade someone to give you what you're asking if they don't like you and trust you.

So how do you gain the trust of a Sugar Daddy in a short amount of time? How do you make a Sugar Daddy to want to help you without coming across as someone needy?

In other words, instead of waiting for others to like you for who you are, why not become a better Sugar Baby? Why not become truly *irresistible* by becoming more skilled, more attractive, and more truly understanding, so they can't wait to help you and provide you what you want?

I'm going to show you how to do exactly that.

Becoming a successful Sugar Baby isn't as simple as reading some script like a magical incantation, but there are *massive* strategic shortcuts you can use to save time.

Plus — what's the alternative? Doing the same thing you've always done? Complaining about how Sugar Daddy dating sites have no good Sugar Daddies? Whining about the over saturation of Sugar Babies?

Let other Sugar Babies whine. *The Sugar Daddy Formula* readers will be busy dominating.

I've systematically studied and tested these techniques for over ten years. Not hand-wavy generic advice that serves up a novel of "Sugar Daddy adventures" but the actual specific ways to conquer your barriers, build a systematic way of deciding what's important, and eliminate distractions.

In fact, I'll show you.

Here's what I'm going to be revealing in this book:

You can either choose to complain about how you aren't finding potential Sugar Daddies, and how the Sugar

Daddy dating site you are on aren't getting you the results you desire.

Or you can play the cards you were dealt, recognize that we all start at different levels, and optimize what you've got.

Others wait to be found by a Sugar Daddy. Successful Sugar Babies become better catches.

Does this sound familiar? "Yeah, I should really do X" (rewrite my profile, take better pictures, work on my goals, work out, or leave a bad Sugar relationship)...but you know it's never going to happen?

My eternal fascination is when Wannabe Sugar Babies say one thing, but do another.

It's time to take the focus off of your problems and think about the man you want to attract. So in the next few chapters, I'm going to show you how to deeply understand your Sugar Daddy.

When you can do this right, you can better understand Sugar Daddies. It's the ultimate way of connecting with Sugar Daddies beyond the perfunctory "Hey, what're you looking for?"

Ladies, let's get to the good stuff.

3 The Sugar Baby Mindset

et's take a moment to clear away some of the nonsense that I'm sure is clogging your brain and preventing you from seeing clearly. Here are four Sugar Baby Misconceptions that you may have:

Sugar Baby Misconception #1: You must have the perfect "privileged background" to appeal to a Sugar Daddy.

Answer: That's a bunch of BS.

Sugar Baby Misconception #2: You can't be a woman of color and be a successful Sugar Baby.

Answer: That idea is just plain stupid.

Sugar Baby Misconception #3: You must be a super-model to attract a Sugar Daddy.

Answer: I know plenty of Sugar Babies who are not supermodels. I'm not a supermodel.

Sugar Baby Misconception #4: You have to be a young woman to be a Sugar Baby.

Answer: Older women can be Sugar Babies. Heck, *all* woman are Sugar Babies.

Ok? Good. Now let's get back to business.

Here's the thing when it comes to Sugar Daddy dating online: a lot of Sugar Babies step into this medium without having the right mindset to make it work for them. And then when it doesn't work for them, they say that online Sugar Daddy dating doesn't work. That's not the case. Online Sugar Daddy dating works for thousands of Sugar Babies. If it's not working for you, there's something you need to figure out.

Now you know that, and that's why you're here. But blaming online Sugar Daddy dating sites for not providing you with a Sugar Daddy is like blaming the gym for not making you lose weight. It's your responsibility to make the most of it. And I'm confident that after reading this book, a lot of lights are going to be going off as to things you could be doing differently.

The smartest thing a Sugar Baby can do is to learn how to master the art and not be judgmental of the very Sugar Babies who are doing exactly what you want to do.

It's remarkable how often that happens. We somehow judge other Sugar Babies as if their pursuit of finding what they want out of this lifestyle is any less sincere than ours.

Going into online Sugar Daddy dating, you need to be able to think long term. This is not a short- term proposition by any stretch of the imagination. When you start thinking of online Sugar Daddy dating as a short-term thing, you're pretty much sealing your own fate.

Think about it in these terms. How many times in your life have you found a man to assist you through his financial generosity? None, twice, three times maybe? The fact is, finding a man to do what you want is a process. It's rare, it's special, and the thought that you should be able to do that within a couple of days on an online Sugar Daddy dating website – well, that would be close to miraculous. It can happen, but to bank on just signing up to a website isn't going to get you a Sugar Daddy to start doing what you want. That's not the way this whole thing plays out.

Being a Sugar Baby is a lifestyle choice and not just a label, and finding a Sugar Daddy online is something to incorporate into your life, just like going to the gym is something to incorporate into your life. It's not some-thing you do for a month and say, "Okay, I'm healthy now. I never have to go to the gym again." I say this to you as a woman who dated online for years and went out with tons of Sugar Daddies. I really try to practice what I preach because I know that as frustrating as it could be at times, this was my ticket – this was my instantaneous way of creating a lifestyle that I wanted from scratch when I couldn't count on a website handing one to me.

And so you must carve out room in your life the way you carve out room to do the things that are important to you. Whatever you do that's important, it has to show up in your effort. Effort is going to be the key to your success in finding the Sugar Daddy you want.

Similarly, when we're talking about building that Sugar Baby mindset and how you're going to conduct yourself in the process of Sugar Daddy dating online, remember that this is a process to be taken seriously. If you took the time to buy the book, you're not here to do a big old email blast in the first week you're on there, or write to every potential Sugar Daddy. That's not smart. That's not patient. That's not methodical.

If you're the kind of person who deletes spam from your computer, so do the very Sugar Daddies that you would like to date. And if you see spamming as the answer to successful online Sugar Daddy dating, for all those Sugar Babies who ever told you it's a numbers game – yes, ultimately you might have to contact, meet, and process a lot of Sugar Daddies in order to find the one. But that doesn't mean when something is a numbers game that you play all the numbers at once.

Yes, you have access to thousands of potential Sugar Daddies online. Don't mistake that for a choice of Sugar Daddies. Just because you see a potential Sugar Daddy doesn't mean you automatically have the ability to get him to go out with you. And if your inclination is to go on to any online Sugar Daddy dating site and write to the twenty-five most appealing Sugar Daddies on that site, you can't get upset if they don't respond. I assure you that unless you're one of the twenty-five most attractive Sugar Babies on the entire website, it's going to be difficult to get the attention of the Sugar Daddies who are appealing to a lot of Sugar Babies.

So once again, access to these Sugar Daddies whom you might not meet in real life – Sugar Daddies who appear to be like the real deal – does not mean you will be going out with them instantly just by showing that you're interested. You shouldn't waste a ton of time worrying about them.

Frankly, this medium brings out the worst in men.

The problem is with the nature of this medium. Sugar Daddies can hide behind their computers and never be held accountable to their actions. This is why men will lie, mislead, disappear, and be rude, crude, and perverted. So what? Those men don't count in your world. When Sugar Daddies exhibit that kind of behavior that just means they've made your decision a lot easier. No point in wasting your time with those kinds of Sugar Daddies. Rest assured there are genuine Sugar Daddies on these sites worthy of your time. My job is to show you how to capture the keepers.

It's important to understand the difference between someone who is rude and someone who is acting in his self-interest. If someone doesn't write back to you, it doesn't necessarily mean they're rude. If they tell you off, they're rude. We have to be able to distinguish those two things. We're going to be doing a lot of that in this book. It's all about understanding why Sugar Daddies do what they do and how not to take it personally. How to understand that you're responsible for your behavior and how to walk away from the things that are not working for you.

To succeed in the long run takes three things: patience, creative Sugar Baby marketing, and understanding your Sugar Daddy. Patience is simply because this takes time. There are no two ways about it. Unless lightning strikes, you're going to be doing this for a while.

Then again, I can tell you the story of someone who, on the first date, found her Sugar Daddy. So don't get too stuck on the bad stories, just understand that more likely than not you're going to have to get good at this process. Once again, it's just like getting good at working out and incorporating it into your life.

Be patient. Sugar Daddies did not make their money in a day, and very rarely do Sugar Babies sign up on a dating site and say, "I got what I came for, thank you very much, good bye," all in the same day.

The second thing that's essential to the online Sugar Daddy dating process is your Sugar Baby marketing. That's actually the hard part. You're going to have to target your potential Sugar Daddy and get him to perceive you to be the one for him. No worries; I've got that covered in the book.

This medium and the people in the medium can be shallow and they can be cruel, and most of our frustration occurs when we think we deserve to date Sugar Daddies who don't want to date us. Therefore, realistic expectations need to be set for your online Sugar Daddy dating process.

If you're a hot young bombshell, you've got it made. But the rest of us, to some degree, better buckle up for a bumpy ride. And that's where self-confidence comes in. Because, statistically speaking, you're going to be rejected.

Now don't take the concept of rejection personally. We're going to spend plenty of time talking about it. It's not personal. It's never personal. It's simply the fact that everybody seems to feel they have so many choices that they're justified in not writing back to you.

The majority of Sugar Daddies with whom you initiate contact are not going to write back. And it doesn't mean a thing. Just be understanding of this fact. You cannot blame the Sugar Daddy or whine about his choices. If a Sugar Baby gets upset because a man doesn't want to date a particular ethnicity and she spends a lot of time dwelling on that, she'll be perpetually depressed. She just doesn't understand how online dating works.

Rejection is part of the process, and what we have to do is learn how to minimize what rejection means. I've been rejected more times than I can count. Due to how long I've done this and how much energy I've put into it, I'm sure I've been rejected more than you have. I'm still standing. I'm a happy Sugar Baby and I'm living the lifestyle I want. I made it through and I had a lot of great online Sugar Daddy dating experiences and adventures.

So every time I tell you something, this is stuff I had to learn the hard way. And I really want to save you the trouble of having to learn my way — or worse, not learn at all.

I know I'm hitting you up front with a whole bunch of things that don't always sound rosy. I feel that's my responsibility towards you — not just to paint the happiest picture of how this thing works. Because if I paint you the happy picture and then you step into this world and it doesn't turn out that way, then you feel even worse, like it's just you who's going through this. Trust me, it's everybody. So once again understand the rules of how this thing works. You're going to have a better experience than if you were surprised. This is why it's my job to give you all the rough stuff up front so you know what to expect and you can really make the most of it.

And listen: from me to you, if you find a better way of Sugar Daddy dating, then do it. Don't complain that online Sugar Daddy dating sucks and there's a lot of rejection.

The number one question I get: "Where do you meet good Sugar Daddies?" It's a no-brainer. You can find them online. They're looking for a mutually beneficial relationship just like you. They're everywhere and they're wondering how to connect with you. In my book, all men are potential Sugar Daddies, and it's a matter of finding the one you want who will provide you with your wants and needs.

This doesn't mean you can't find them offline. By being an online Sugar Daddy dating advocate, I'm not suggesting that this is the only game in town. I'm saying that this platform puts you within reach of potential Sugar Daddies to whom you otherwise have no access.

I have Sugar Babies who reach out to me telling me how nobody was writing to them, and then with a few changes to what they were currently doing got three dates lined up. That's the way this thing goes.

How do we not make our lows so low? How do we not ride this rollercoaster and get sick because some weeks are better, and sometimes you're feeling a little more confident and better about this process than others. The ups and downs are part of the process and the downs aren't really that down. They're just a slight drought that always turns around.

As much as you probably like to think there are better ways of meeting Sugar Daddies, there aren't. There literally are no better ways of meeting potential Sugar Daddies than online. It's inexpensive, you can do it any time of day, there is no need to go out, and you don't have to get dressed up. You've got the ability to market yourself, and to say a whole bunch of things about yourself that appeal to others in a way you couldn't possibly do anywhere else. You've got the ability to screen anonymously, and the ability to search and filter before you even go out with them. The more you put into this, the more you'll get out. Having the right Sugar Baby mindset is essential for you to make the most of online Sugar Daddy dating.

Now let's sum up what we just covered in this section. It's the Sugar Baby Mindset review.

Finding a Sugar Daddy online can put us in touch with potential Sugar Daddies much more quickly than any other method. As much as we would like to think that we can attract all Sugar Daddies, we won't. It's just the reality of it. Conversely, we will not be attracted to all Sugar Daddies. It's okay. The bottom line is that rejection is a normal part of the Sugar Baby process. Expect it. Manage it. Own it. Whining and bashing the Sugar Daddy who rejected you is a great way to get stuck in the cycle of failure. It's just another way of protecting your ego – and there's no way you can possibly learn what you need to learn to become your best Sugar Baby possible.

If you don't think this lifestyle is for you, then why should a Sugar Daddy want to date you? Reread that. And reread that again. No excuses. In order to figure out why you're not getting the results that you're seeking, you have to take a look at what is wrong.

If you are already on a Sugar Daddy website, take a moment to answer some basic questions.

- If you're finding only potential Sugar Daddies who are looking for a quick weekend fling, ask yourself how you're coming across in your profile. Be honest with yourself. Are you writing to attract a high-quality Sugar Daddy?

- How do your pictures look? What image are you painting in the eyes of your potential Sugar Daddy?

- What about your headline? Does it stand out from the rest? Does it make you curious to want to know more about you?

- Can you answer this: Why would a Sugar Daddy date you? Establish your "Sugar Baby Allure," which is what will make you more attractive to the ones you want.

- Are you on the right site? Not all sites are created equal.

- If your Sugar Daddy dating method isn't working, change the direction (but not the goal) of the reason why you want to be a Sugar Baby!

Ok? We're ready to move on to the next section, where we're really going to dive into the nitty-gritty.

Part Two:
The Sugar Daddy Formula

4 Your Sugar Daddy Blueprint

B efore we begin, I want you to know that I don't want you to feel overwhelmed with all that you need to do to create a profile. You can start on one area and then keep tweaking certain aspects until you find what works for you. The main thing is to start with your goals and attract the Sugar Daddy that you want. You don't have to conquer the world — just one man.

Let's get down to business. You know that finding, meeting and seducing mature and generous Sugar Daddies isn't exactly a walk in the park. After all, let's think about all the obstacles you need to overcome. There's

25

signing up for the right Sugar Daddy dating website and setting up a profile that sings. There's the challenge of attracting the exact type of Sugar Daddies you're looking for (and avoiding the scammers!), tempting them to respond to your profile, and writing the kind of responses that seduce them right then and there.

Then there's the hurdle of meeting up with them and striking the right note between sophisticated and seductive. Additionally, you need to be able to quickly identify your Sugar Daddy's personality type, so you can tailor your conversation specifically so you can seduce him through your words.

And let's not forget everything you need to go through once you've managed to seduce your Sugar Daddy. For example, how do you keep him coming back for more? What do you do when you want him to assist with his financial generosity? How do you keep things fresh and interesting so he'll always want to keep you around?

Is your head spinning yet?

Luckily, you don't have to struggle through the world of complicated Sugar Daddy dating alone – because *The Sugar Daddy Formula Blueprint* is here to guide you through it all!

I want you to think of this book as a map through the winding and twisting roads of Sugar Daddy dating.

There are three parts to this. Parts one and two are about the Sugar Daddy Formula, which will give you a simple eight-step formula that I have used over and over again to find and attract the best Sugar Daddy for me. My clients have taken this formula, plugged in their own preferences, and achieved the exact same results.

Part three is all about getting what you want out of your Sugar Daddy relationship. Most Sugar Babies that I meet don't know what they're doing. They get into relationships where they're giving their Sugar Daddy everything *he* wants without getting anything *they* want.

After reading part three, you will not have this problem!

Putting all of this together, what are some of the specific things you will learn this book?

- You'll discover how to set up the foundations for your ultimate Sugar Baby success;

- You'll uncover the secrets of creating the kind of profile and responses that make Sugar Daddies line up to meet you;

- You'll reveal how to transition your online relationship into the real world;

- You'll learn how to create a seductive aura of mystery that will leave him begging for more;

- You'll discover just how to keep your Sugar Daddy coming around;

- You'll learn just how to ask for what you want from your Sugar Daddy;

- You'll uncover the exact techniques you need to use to grow your Sugar Daddy relationship;

As you can see, this book is a must-have guide that no Sugar Baby should go without!

Before we get into the Sugar Baby Formula, let's talk for a minute about one of the biggest misconceptions about being a Sugar Baby? That's an easy one: it's that only girls with supermodel looks can ever be a Sugar Baby. Blame popular media for this perception. With so many movies, music videos and television shows promoting the idea that Sugar Babies use their looks in order to get gifts and money from their men, it's no wonder that most of society believes that only incredibly beautiful women can be Sugar Babies. But the best Sugar Babies aren't supermodels; heck, many of them look like the average girl down the street! So what makes these girls so successful, despite having "average" looks?

- They know how to laugh. Ever noticed that people tend to gravitate around those who are happy and positive? The same works with Sugar Babies and Sugar Daddies. The most successful

Sugar Babies are those who always have a smile on their face and are ready to laugh.

- They have an opinion. Women who use their looks to get things don't realize just how invaluable an opinion can be. Wealthy and powerful men may appreciate a beautiful woman, but they really enjoy being around an intelligent woman who has an educated opinion.

- They're honest about their intentions. The best Sugar Babies know that an open line of communication is crucial to the success of their relationships. From their financial expectations to their goals for the relationships, Sugar Babies know that the more honest they are about what they want from the relationship, the more successful it will be.

When it comes to being a Sugar Baby, you don't need to be a supermodel to land a top-quality Sugar Daddy — you just need to be yourself!

5 Getting Started

Taking that first step into Sugar Daddy dating is always the hardest. It's okay to admit it: you have no idea what you're doing. After all, there are so many questions to ask and so many things to remember. It's enough to make anyone want to run away and hide from the Sugar Baby journey.

But not you. Because you've got a secret on your side...

My eight-step Sugar Daddy Formula, which can be implemented over the course of just a few weeks!

That's right: in just a few weeks, you can meet the Sugar Daddy of your dreams and be well on your way towards experiencing the Sugar Baby lifestyle you've been dreaming about!

Ready to make it happen? Of course you are. I'm taking what I've learned from my experience and applying it to your Sugar Daddy dating experience!

I know what you're thinking right now: How did you find success so quickly? And will I achieve the same results?

Great question.

First, let me point out what most Wannabe Sugar Babies are doing...and why it's taking them so long to find high-quality Sugar Daddies (if they ever do!) Here are the steps they take:

Step One: Find a Sugar Daddy site.

Step Two: Write a profile and post a sexy picture.

Step Three: Wait and hope to capture many high-class Sugar Daddies.

Step Four: Watch the traffic die and then cancel the account.

Step Five: Find a new Sugar Daddy dating site to post the profile and repeat.

Want to know how to do things differently if you want to attract the Sugar Daddy of your dreams in as little as two weeks...like I did? Here's how I start my Sugar Daddy dating, and how you should too:

Step One: Write Down Your Goals

First, identify what you want out of your Sugar Baby experience, and what kind of Sugar Daddy you want to spend your time with. A lot of Wannabe Sugar Babies skip over this part because they think it's obvious, and they soon regret it!

Step Two: Configure Your Sugar Baby Story

The story of your life is one of the most interesting things you'll ever possess – and you'll be surprised at how you can lure in a Sugar Daddy with your Sugar Baby story. If you're not playing up your story to make it exciting and intriguing, then you're truly missing out on a wonderful opportunity.

Step Three: Craft a Profile to Attract the Sugar Daddy You Want

If you want a specific type of Sugar Daddy then you want to write specifically for him. Not all Sugar Daddies will be a good fit for you as they may not be on the same page as to what you are looking for. Quality is far better than quantity. It's harder and it takes more work for you to choose the right words, but it's an entirely worthwhile investment in time.

Step Four: Craft an "Auto-Reply Response," Then Tailor It to the Potential Sugar Daddy When You Use It

Think using templates and scripts to appeal to Sugar Daddies is manipulative or "scammy"? It's not – this is a false reaction that many Sugar Babies have as a defense mechanism. It's about using your time wisely. You'll find examples of my "auto-reply responses" in the auto-reply chapter.

Step Five: Chose a Site That Will Accelerate Your Search for Your Dream Sugar Daddy

Not all Sugar Daddy dating sites are created equal... so find the dating site that meets your needs, and post your profile there. If you screw this step up, then following the other steps to the letter cannot save you. After all, if you don't put yourself in front of qualified Sugar Daddies you are wasting your time!

Step Six: Select a Picture That Adds to Your Story

Invest in an amazing picture. Do not post a grainy snapshot from your friend's bridal shower. Make sure your photos are flattering and inviting. When you pick pictures make sure you have a reason in doing so. Not just because they're sexy but they should add to your story. How do you want your potential Sugar Daddy to view you? Just remember: don't post pictures of yourself in a bikini or making "duck face" at a club. Do not show any men in your photo or you with your girlfriends. These are universal no-nos on Sugar Daddy dating sites!

Step Seven: Craft Your Headline

How you write the headlines for your profile make the difference between Sugar Daddies reading your personal ad or ignoring it completely and the pictures that you use. Be sure to read up on creating profile headlines in chapter nine.

Step Eight: Split Test Your Ads

Those who follow my advice know that I am a huge advocate of split testing your personal ads. Change one sentence and double your response rate.

Strategy + Schedule = Sugar Baby Success.

The difference between what most Sugar Babies do and what I do is my "step one."

Someone else's "step one" and my "step eight." That's where the difference comes in. They're focusing on the wrong variables of what's going to make their Sugar Baby lifestyle a successful one. They're actually working on the exact opposite of what they should be working on. They spend all of their time convincing Sugar Daddies of what they hope to gain out of the relationship, rather than focusing on the needs of their Sugar Daddy and getting them to want to help them succeed.

So, in much shorter words… make yourself indispensable to your Sugar Daddy and let your profile do your Sugar Baby marketing for you.

Some Sugar Babies assume that it's just luck. It's not just the site that you are on that makes the difference. It's your profile. While other Sugar Babies write mediocre profiles, I stand out. That's been the main way I've differentiated myself from the rest of the Sugar Babies.

What is one thing most aspiring Sugar Babies are doing wrong that is holding them back?

They focus on what they hope to get out of the relationship and not about how they are going to go about getting it.

Sugar Daddy dating can be an exciting lifestyle if you go about it the right way. And if you plug in my simple formula, you're bound to meet a high-quality Sugar Daddy in just a few weeks!

Now that you know the basics of the Sugar Daddy Formula, I am going to spend the next nine chapters laying out each step in detail so that you know exactly what to do at every step of the way.

6 Know What You Want

Setting goals is crucial to your Sugar Baby success. Sugar Baby goals give you a clear direction of where you need to go in order to enjoy Sugar Baby success. Without goals, you're at risk of wasting your time on a Sugar Daddy who may seem nice, but isn't ultimately the right fit.

That's why developing basic Sugar Baby goals is so crucial to the overall experience. If you don't define what you're looking for, and the expectations aren't set, then you'll run into a lot of misunderstandings.

On the other hand, setting basic goals and expectations in the beginning of your journey will help you realize what you're prepared to do, and what you need to draw the line at.

And once you understand these key points, you can effectively communicate them to your Sugar Daddy so he knows what to expect as well.

It's a win-win scenario for everyone!

Here is the magic question:

Why Do You Want to Become a Sugar Baby?

Stop and think about this for a bit. You need a good reason as to why you're doing this. Otherwise, you won't make it very far.

You need to have a clear direction of where you're going before you can get there. That's where these key Sugar Baby questions come in:

- How much effort are you willing to put into your Sugar Baby journey? Will you be doing this once a week, a few times a week, or every day?

- How intimate do you want to get with your Sugar Daddy, and how quickly do you want that to happen? No, I'm not necessarily talking about sex here, although that's key too. I'm talking about a deeper more lasting connection with your Sugar Daddy.

- Are you prepared to deal with the emotional connotations of becoming a Sugar Baby? For example, some men may view you as a prostitute – are you ready to handle that?

- How much of an emotional commitment do you want to make?

- What's your timeline to devote to this?

- Do you want one Sugar Daddy, or multiple?

As you can see, if you really want the Sugar Baby lifestyle, you must be prepared to devote some serious time and energy if you are to be successful.

I ask this question of other Sugar Babies a lot, and I often hear a response like, "I just want to make some extra cash on the side."

That is a vague, hand-wavy answer that is more pointed toward an escort than a Sugar Baby lifestyle.

After receiving hundreds of emails from Sugar Babies, I can count on one hand those who really impressed me with their vision. I can almost see the look of determination in their faces. Sometimes their motivation stems from a negative event: "Taylor, I'm doing this because I have to make this work or I'm going to be out on the street next month." And sometimes it's positive: "I want to experience the world and meet a man who will help me realize my dreams of starting my own business." (That's where I was when I got started on my own Sugar Baby journey.)

Do you see the difference between those strong statements and the wishy-washy, hand-wavy answers most

Sugar Babies give? I do. Your vague answer is a dead giveaway that you'd be wasting your time on your Sugar Baby journey. Harsh? Perhaps this is a reality check you need.

Whether your motivations are personal or world changing, you need to be 100% in the game if you're going to be a success as a Sugar Baby. If you're sitting around right now wondering how you can make an extra couple of hundred dollars a month, I'm going to stand up and shout this at you right now: Your goals aren't big enough.

Somewhere between "building your empire" and "being a Sugar Baby with goals" is where you want to start.

But don't you have to start somewhere? Take whatever your goal was and make it ten times bigger. Then start there. That'll get you out of bed!

Goal Setting: Planning to Live Your Sugar Baby Life Your Way

The following broad guidelines will help you to set effective, achievable Sugar Baby goals:

State each goal as a positive statement. Express your goals positively – "I know I'm going to find a high-quality Sugar Daddy" is a much better goal than "I hope I don't end up making a fool of myself."

Be precise. Set precise goals, putting in dates, times and amounts so that you can measure achievement. If you do this, you'll know exactly when you have achieved the goal, and can take complete satisfaction from having achieved it.

Set priorities. When you have several goals, give each a priority. This helps you to avoid feeling over-whelmed by having too many Sugar Baby goals, and helps to direct your attention to the most important ones.

Write goals down. This crystallizes them and gives them more force.

Keep operational goals small. Keep the low-level goals that you're working towards small and achievable. If a goal is too large, then it can seem that you are not making progress towards it. Keeping goals small and incremental gives more opportunities for reward.

Set performance goals, not outcome goals. You should take care to set goals over which you have as much control as possible.

Set realistic goals. It's important to set goals that you can achieve. Even other Sugar Babies can set unrealistic goals for you. They will often do this in ignorance of your own desires and ambitions with flashing what they have in hopes of achieving what they got.

Remember that your goals will change as time goes on. Adjust them regularly to reflect growth in your knowledge and experience, and if goals do not hold any attraction any longer, consider letting them go.

A Sugar Baby Example for Setting Goals

For her Sugar Baby resolution, Susan has decided to think about what she really wants to achieve out of the SB lifestyle.

Her lifetime goals are as follows:

Career - "To own my own art gallery in the city."

Artistic - "To keep working on my illustration skills. Ultimately I want to have my own show in our downtown gallery."

Physical - "To run a marathon."

Now that Susan has listed her lifetime goals, she then breaks down each one into smaller, more manageable goals. Let's take a closer look at how she might break down her lifetime career goal – owning her own art gallery:

Lifetime Goal: Own My Own Art Gallery

Five-year goal: "Be a successful art gallery owner thanks to an initial investment by my Sugar Daddy."

One-year goal: "To have myself be supported by a Sugar Daddy who is interested in a long-term relationship with me."

Six-month goal: "Meet at least five high-quality Sugar Daddies that I can imagine being in a Sugar Daddy/Sugar Baby relationship with."

One-month goal: "Join a Sugar Daddy dating website and upload my profile."

One-week goal: "Research the best Sugar Daddy dating sites online."

As you can see from this example, breaking big goals down into smaller, more manageable goals makes it far easier to see how the goal will get accomplished.

More Key Points to Setting a Sugar Baby Goal

Let's take a look at another example to really highlight how to set a Sugar Baby goal. Let's say you want to start a business and need financial help from your Sugar Daddy.

Here's how you would approach breaking down that goal:

✓ What do you plan on using the funds for?

✓ Introduce the topic of what you are seeking via email. This gives your Sugar Daddy time to think over the proposition without feeling pressured.

✓ Give your Sugar Daddy the chance to bring it up during the next phone call or date. You don't want to immediately bombard him, as this will make him feel defensive. However, be prepared from the very start of your interactions with a perspective Sugar Daddy to discuss what you are looking for he may bring it up.

✓ If your Sugar Daddy doesn't bring it up, mention it yourself.

To help supplement your goal-achieving powers, you'll want to use these key tips:

• Be positive, no matter what happens. Whining won't help you achieve anything.

• Set your bottom line for a monthly allowance. If your Sugar Daddy won't agree to this bottom line, let him know you're willing to walk away from the relationship.

• Give him reasons to want to help you. These could include reminding him that you're worth it, or that you'll use the extra money to start your own business or attend college.

To help you achieve this example goal, here's an opening statement you could use in the email or on the phone to ask for an allowance:

> "Hi _____ {insert Sugar Daddy name}, I hope you're doing well! I just wanted to let you know that I've been thinking about _____ {insert what you plan on using the funds for}, and I've decided that _____ dollars would be a suitable amount. I want to use the money to _____ {insert goal}, and I know you'll be glad to help out, as you have been so generous with your time. Let's talk about it during our next date, as I'm sure you have a lot of questions."

Yes, I want you to have a script in front of you when you make the call and you should practice beforehand too.

See? It really is as simple as that!

Remember, the key to your success as a Sugar Baby is to lay down a map for where you want this incredible journey to take you. Being a Sugar Baby is undeniably fun, but the real thrill from the experience is getting what you want and you in the driver's seat steering straight for your goals – be it a new business venture or the financial security that gives you more peace of mind.

Sugar Baby Goal Setting Activity #1: Clarify Your Vision

Do you have a vision of what you want to achieve out of this lifestyle?

Write a paragraph describing how you envision this life-style going and what you want and how you plan to use the generosity of your Sugar Daddy to help you.

Sugar Baby Goal Setting Activity #2: Prioritize Your Sugar Baby Goals

When you think of the many areas of your life it is like-ly that you may have a number of goals. Make a list of all the goals that you have set — and list them in pri-ority. This will help when "Asking for what you want from your Sugar Daddy." When you have a clearer idea of your goals it makes it easier to ask!

Make a list of all the goals that you have set. (*Do not exceed eight.*)

1.

2.

3.

4.

5.

6.

7.

8.

7 Create Your Sugar Baby Story

The story of your life is one of the most interesting things you'll ever possess – and you'll be surprised at how you can lure in a Sugar Daddy with your Sugar Baby story. If you're not playing up your story to make it exciting and intriguing, then you're truly missing out on a wonderful opportunity.

Learning how to tell the perfect Sugar Baby story can entice, inspire, stimulate, or fascinate a potential Sugar Daddy – but you cannot *make* a Sugar Daddy listen. Embracing this fact up front lets us focus on what we *can* do. We can create curiosity. Influencing is a function of grabbing someone's attention, connecting to what they already feel is important, and linking that feeling to whatever you want them to see, do, or feel.

To prepare, you can develop the basic skills of communicating with the only instrument of communication available to you: you. When you tell a story, your body and your voice become the stage. Finding the right story to tell may take some effort. However, your effort to connect before you try to convince will be rewarded. Too many Wannabe Sugar Babies outline the relationship in what they hope to receive out of it and waste effort because they focus on their own needs before establishing a connection. Without a bridge between you and your potential Sugar Daddies, all of your words fall into the gap between you. When we assume that Sugar Daddies already know what we want, we sabotage our own ability to influence – and the Sugar Daddies you want to influence have already formed an opinion about you and your intentions. Once you have connected, you are ready to move your potential Sugar Daddy, step by step, to see the world as you see it and put you in a better position of getting what you want.

How to Stand Out from Thousands of Other Sugar Babies

How are you going to be remembered when there are thousands of Sugar Babies vying for the same Sugar Daddies' attention?

Your "Sugar Baby Story" is an art.

It's designed to get Sugar Daddies to ask you more information about you. It's designed for you to quickly be able to convey to your Sugar Daddy who you are in a captivation way – thus making your time spent on it insanely profitable.

When you seek to influence Sugar Daddies you face three pivotal questions, which include the following:

1. What's your Sugar Baby story?

2. Who are you?

3. Where are you heading and what are your Goals?

Your Sugar Baby Story can be used to persuade, motivate, and inspire Sugar Daddies to doing what you want – but only if you know how to use it.

Just because you label yourself a Sugar Baby isn't going to get you what you want out of this lifestyle. Genuine influence goes deeper than getting Sugar Daddies to do what you want them to. It means gaining their trust... And that's exactly where your Sugar Baby story comes into play.

First, Know Thyself

No matter who you are or where you come from, as a Sugar Baby, you fall into one of four Sugar Baby categories:

1. **Mercenary Sugar Baby.** Mercenary is just another word for a Sugar Baby who's just looking for financial benefits from her Sugar Daddy. From getting that tuition bill paid to using credit cards with virtually no limits, the Mercenary Sugar Baby is looking to make stacks of cash.

2. **Sugar Baby Opportunist.** This Sugar Baby is looking to benefit both emotionally and financially. She wants a Sugar Daddy that won't just take care of her bills, but can provide her with a fulfilling emotional relationship as well.

3. **Sugar Baby Enhancer.** This Sugar Baby is looking to live the high life without receiving any financial benefits. She already has the money to treat herself to what she wants – she just wants the right man to open those exclusive restaurant and club doors!

4. **Traditional Sugar Baby.** She's looking to meet with Sugar Daddies to form deep emotional connections and have a fulfilling relationship with her Sugar Daddy.

So why is it so important to understand which Sugar Baby personality type you fall under? The reasoning is simple: once you understand more about your Sugar Baby personality, you can better communicate your needs and expectations to your Sugar Daddy.

Understanding what exactly you want from your Sugar Daddy is crucial to ensuring that you actually get it. For example, if you're a Mercenary Sugar Baby but you keep finding Sugar Daddies who would rather open exclusive doors than their wallets to you, then knowing that you want financial gifts will help you narrow down better Sugar Daddies for your needs. Conversely, it can also help you better communicate with your Sugar Daddy about what you expect, and what you don't particularly care for.

If the thought of being so upfront with your Sugar Daddy about what gifts you expect from him makes you cringe, not to worry: you don't have to be so forthright with the information. All you have to do is find a void that's missing in his life, and determine how you can fulfill that void. While it might seem a bit depressing, choosing a Sugar Daddy who has something missing from his life will give you an opportunity to fill that void and is the best way to guarantee the success of your relationship.

As an example, I used to have a Sugar Daddy who was an absolute workaholic. He loved working late, and weekends were just extra days that could be spent on take-home work. I found that what was missing in his life was a companion who was understanding of his lifestyle, and who would be ready and waiting when he wanted to have some fun.

Knowing your Sugar Baby type is crucial to making your Sugar Baby story. Let's talk about that now.

Envisioning Long-Term Sugar Daddy Relationships

Your Sugar Baby Story is your path to a long-term Sugar Daddy. Sugar Daddies value their own conclusions more highly than yours. They will only believe in your Sugar Baby Story if it has become real for them personally. Gain their trust, and future influence will require very little effort.

Developing those Sugar Daddies you wish to influence begins with two major questions that you need to answer about yourself:

1. Who are you?

2. Why are you here?

Before you attempt to influence any Sugar Daddy you need to establish enough trust to deliver your message.

Since you don't have time to build trust within a short time period you can best do this through your Sugar Baby Story. A story lets them decide for themselves. If your story is good enough, Sugar Daddies – of their own free will – come to the conclusion they can trust you.

How can you expect Sugar Daddies to trust you and be influenced by you when they don't know who you are? Your Sugar Baby Story is key to getting what you want.

Here's a set of rules for crafting your Sugar Baby Story from your profile and quickly turning yourself into a memorable Sugar Baby.

Rule 1: Never Start With "I"

Why's this, you might ask? Simple: you want to snap your Sugar Daddies out of a trance and get them to start paying attention to your online profile. And your Sugar Baby profile is not about you. It's not about saying "I'm this, I'm that." Rather, it's about appealing to and seducing potential Sugar Daddies through the power of your words. Essentially, the only goal is to capture the interest of the potential Sugar Daddy you want. Period.

When it's finally time to introduce yourself via email to a potential Sugar Daddy, you have to know some of his deepest desires. Here's a hint that will give you a massive head start: Their deepest desire isn't to set up a "mutual arrangement." So scratch out "Are you seeking a mutual arrangement?" as a question!

I start out with a simple question: "Do you want to be the cigar to my lips?" And then I let the mystery build onto my profile, and that mystery makes a curious Sugar Daddy respond to your personal ad.

You'll notice some reactions when you do this and more clicks to your ad. Some Sugar Daddies will grin and respond with a witty response. The point is, however, that you're receiving responses. And the more responses you receive, the more likely it is that you'll find your dream Sugar Daddy.

Rule 2: Incorporate This Unstoppable Formula For Creating a Compelling Sugar Baby Story

Your Sugar Baby Story needs to contain these elements:

1. Compelling value.

2. A call to action.

3. What you need from your Sugar Daddy (mentor, confidante, business insight, or financial acumen).

Sounds kind of like writing a sales letter, doesn't it?

I concede that your Sugar Baby story may be even more difficult. You have to quickly identify your Sugar Daddy's most compelling value proposition and present it.

Here's an unstoppable formula that will help you create a Sugar Baby story so powerful, your Sugar Daddy won't be able to resist contacting you:

{Sugar Baby Allure} + {Desirable Outcome} = {Curious Sugar Daddy}

The Sugar Baby Allure would be your passion for something. For example music, reading, or any other hobby you might have, and how it makes you feel. Once you've established this allure, then you want to take your Sugar Daddy with you and draw him in and make him get to know you.

That makes a Sugar Daddy respond to you – and I promise that when used correctly this formula never fails.

I like a man who smokes a cigar. They are in a certain class and this goes to their income brackets, and I too like cigars.

Remember the line I used above, about how I want my Sugar Daddy to be the cigar to my lips? Here's the rest of the email message:

"I love to unwind with an occasional cigar. It's like tasting a good wine: you smell it, you taste it, you look at it, you feel it – you can even hear it. *(Now I would write something flirty to him).* Let me be the cigar to your lips and take you away to a place of undying pleasure. The warmth of me will dwell in your mind. Come inside my world and let me make you feel that special place that only I possess. For within me lies the fire that makes you want to consume me. Can you feel me?"

Yes, it seems a bit over the top at first, but trust me, no Sugar Daddy will be able to resist you once he reads these words.

Rule 3: Hone Your Story By Watching Sugar Daddy Responses

As I say my pitch, I watch the response that I receive from my potential Sugar Daddies. I'm looking for a re-action, and I'm most interested in surprise reactions, as these mean the Sugar Daddy is listening and is more likely to remember me.

The best reaction is when a Sugar Daddy replies with more of an intellectual thought-out response. That's the verbal equivalent of me capturing their interest: hook, line, and sinker! I have achieved the desired effect. And believe me, quality matters more than quantity.

Being a Sugar Baby isn't easy, and although we like to think that we can attract any Sugar Daddy, we won't; and not all Sugar Daddies are going to appeal to us. It's just the reality of it.

Just stay true to yourself and you will find exactly what you are looking for.

A key to changing your Sugar Baby story is watching the Sugar Daddies' reaction to it. With practice, you will learn to tell exactly which words or phrases tune them in and tune them out. Practice every word of your story, and tweak constantly. Try new things. You have very little to lose and a whole lot to gain.

By designing your Sugar Baby story, then using the elements above, you will be far more memorable. That's the power of a great story. Use my template. It works for me; it will work for just about anyone.

It will definitely make you stand out in an overcrowded world and take you one step closer to fulfilling your Sugar Baby lifestyle!

Sugar Daddy Story Worksheet

Just because you label yourself a Sugar Baby isn't going to get you what you want out of this lifestyle. Genuine influence goes deeper than getting Sugar Daddies to do what you want them to. It means gaining their trust.

The story of your life is one of the most interesting things you'll ever possess — and you'll be surprised at how you can lure in a Sugar Daddy with your Sugar Baby story. If you're not playing up your story to make it exciting and intriguing, then you're truly missing out on a wonderful opportunity.

Your Sugar Baby Story can be used to persuade, motivate, and inspire Sugar Daddies to do what you want — but only if you know how to use it.

And that's exactly where your Sugar Baby story comes into play.

Remember that your Sugar Baby story needs to contain these three elements:

1. Compelling value.

2. A call to action.

3. What you need from your Sugar Daddy (mentor, confidante, business insight or financial acumen).

This worksheet gives you the opportunity to answer these three questions. What's your Sugar Baby story? Who is your ideal Sugar Daddy? You want to understand the type of Sugar Daddy You want and appeal to him. When seeking out the Sugar Daddy you want. You want to align yourself with a Sugar Daddy that will help you achieve your goals faster. Focus your story on capturing his attention.

So, what's your story? Write it here:

Who are you? Why are you here? Where are you heading — what are your goals?

Being on a Sugar Daddy dating site, potential Sugar Daddies may already have a preconceived notation about you. Are you an escort or a golddigger? It is in our human nature to expect that anyone out to influence others has something to gain. Most Sugar Daddies subconsciously assume that your gain will mean their loss. You need to tell a story that demonstrates you are the kind of Sugar Baby they can trust, and change their focus on how they perceive you from the beginning. You want to take your goals and frame them in a way to get Sugar Daddies to want to help you. For example, wanting to go back to school is better than wanting to update your wardrobe.

So, who are you and why are you here? Write it here:

Practice, practice, and practice your story so that it feels natural to you, because if you believe your own story, your Sugar Daddy will too! Your words and your voice both play a part. Make sure that they work for you and not against you. Practice in front of a mirror.

8 Where to Find Sugar Daddies

Now that you have taken the time to create your Sugar Daddy goals and have created a compelling Sugar Daddy story that aligns with those goals, you're ready to actually go out and get a Sugar Daddy.

That brings up the million-dollar question: where?

There are a lot of places to meet Sugar Daddies, and I am about to talk about some of them. Ultimately, however, I believe that meeting Sugar Daddies on the internet is the best option out there. That is what the rest of the book will be about.

Nevertheless, I do want to at least give you an idea of what your other possibilities are. After all, there were plenty of Sugar Babies finding Sugar Daddies before the internet came around!

Ideal Locations (and Websites) for Hunting and Catching Your Very Own Sugar Daddy

When it comes to being a successful Sugar Baby, there's no denying that you'll have to take your destiny in your own hands. Rather than waiting around in cocktail bars for wealthy-looking men to approach you (and even then, there's no guarantee that they're the Sugar Daddies you're looking for), you need to take the initiative and hunt down the right Sugar Daddy to fulfill your Sugar Baby needs.

Well, get ready to stand up and cheer, because I'm about to reveal something totally unexpected to you. Rather than going for the obvious locations to hunt down your Sugar Daddy – and those trendy cocktail bars are one of them! – it's time to start thinking outside the box...

...And start putting yourself in the shoes of your Sugar Daddy!

With regards to the ideal locations to find your Sugar Daddy, you need to remind yourself that your Sugar Daddy is a wealthy and powerful man. Unless he magically inherited a great deal of money from his family, it's likely that his wealth came from a combination of some serious work ethic, charisma and dedication to his business. Therefore, it's unlikely that he's going to blow it all away at the hottest clubs or visit hotel bars. That's just not the typical Sugar Daddy style.

However, I'd like to highlight something crucial here – his work ethic. A successful Sugar Daddy doesn't know when to stop working – and if you want to find one who can make your Sugar Baby dreams come true, then you need to stake out his territory. Don't go to bars or clubs in wealthy neighborhoods; instead, narrow down your vantage point to bars, lounges and gyms near financial districts or other areas of business.

For example, I had one friend who kept going to a high-end bar to find a Sugar Daddy, only to be met by loser guys who were all flash and no cash. So when a new gym opened up in an a massive business district) in a nearby city, she decided to join up. Lo and behold, she was suddenly meeting tons of wealthy businessmen who were popping in at the gym during lunch breaks and directly after work. And because these men weren't in the midst of discussing business with colleagues (which can often happen at bars, lounges and restaurants), she was able to capture their full attention.

Now she has more Sugar Daddies than she knows what to do with!

The point I want to make here is that if you want to hunt down a Sugar Daddy, you need to think like one. Where is he most likely to hang out after work – a trendy club, or a sleek bar that's right outside his office? Is he more likely to hit a gym near his work or near his residence (hint: nine times out of ten, it's the first option)?

Need a little extra push in ideal locations to hunt down your Sugar Daddy? Here are a few hotspots where Sugar Babies often report meeting their Sugar Daddies:

1. Online (This is definitely the way to go – and I'll explain my reasons why below!)

2. Business district bar;

3. Gym;

4. Airlines Concierge Club (Delta Sky Club);

5. Hotel concierge rooms;

6. Food or Beer festivals;

7. Charity events;

8. Wine tastings;

9. And outdoor adventure clubs.

10. Casino

Narrow down the search. Looking for a CEO, you could scout around the convention center in your area, country clubs, cigar lounges, meetups (a Sugar Baby should be strategic about it and think outside the box). A Sugar Baby should focus on where the one she would like to date would be and start her search there. Higher-end restaurant bars, business conventions (any convention that your target would go to.... don't focus on hotels if you live in the area as you will only end up being perceived as a callgirl unless you are portraying yourself as conducting business out of town and you are traveling.

If you really want to narrow down your hunting skills and seek out an ideal Sugar Daddy, why not meet them online?

It sounds shocking, but it's true: more Sugar Daddies than ever before are posting ads online in the hopes of meeting great Sugar Babies who can provide them with the companionship they need. It's not just the convenience of meeting Sugar Daddies that makes the online option so fantastic – it's also a great way to avoid any awkward encounters with wealthy men who will be hesitant over your advances.

After all, think about it in terms of his perspective: if you're dressed to the nines and visiting a business district bar – but don't work around there – some men might jump to salacious conclusions.

Sound good to you? I hope so, because in the coming chapters I am going to share the exact step-by-step formula that I use to find and attract Sugar Daddies on internet dating websites.

All you have to do is read the rest of this book, plug in your own goals and personality, and you'll have more

Sugar Daddies competing for your attention than you know what to do with.

The best part is that they will be Sugar Daddies who are <u>right for you</u>. With this method, you will filter those guys out and spend your precious time and energy with guys who can actually give you what you want.

9 Sculpt an Attractive Profile

You may think you have the best profile on your Sugar Daddy dating website. You may think you're the most attractive Wannabe Sugar Baby on the Internet. But if a potential Sugar Daddy doesn't immediately scream, "She's the one for me!" when he lands on your profile, then you're really missing out on a crucial point of Sugar Daddy dating online.

Some of the best Sugar Babies around still have trouble with the observation I'm about to make. They think that getting a dream Sugar Daddy is all about getting as much traffic to their profile as possible. After all, Sugar Daddy dating is a numbers game... and the more visitors to your profile, the more likely it is that you'll get your dream Sugar Daddy.

Right?

Not necessarily. The point of online Sugar Daddy dating isn't just to get as much traffic to your profile as possible. It's to get those Sugar Daddies to *take action* when they read your profile!

If you're not getting responses from your personal ad, this means it failed. Not the Sugar Daddies. Not the Sugar Daddy dating site. None of these failed.

But your Sugar Baby profile crashed and burned.

No, I'm not saying this to be mean. I'm trying to get you to realize that if you're not getting the responses you want from Sugar Daddies, it means you need to keep tweaking and improving your online profile until you do.

I want to share tips with you to get you noticed: that will make those Sugar Daddies practically give themselves whiplash as they rush to respond to your online profile.

*Targeted profiles: If you want a specific type of Sugar Daddy then you want to write specifically for him. Not all Sugar Daddies will be a good fit for you as they may not be on the same page as to what you are looking for. Quality is far better than Quantity. It's harder and it takes more work for you to choose the right words, but it's an entirely worthwhile investment in time.

*Say more with less: Let's get to the point. Your potential Sugar Daddy isn't going to want to read a novel.

You want to capture his attention and get him to respond. That is the goal of your profile. Just by taking a few things about you that are interesting and describing it in away to stimulate him will get him to respond.

*Headlines: Your headline is just as important as your picture. Start with your profile and then come back to your headline and use that as the Intro to your profile. Your headline is a preview and a teaser of more to come.

*Split Test: Those who follow my advice know that I am a huge advocate of split testing your personal ads. Change one sentence, double your response rate.

*Track conversions: I can't tell you how many Sugar Babies find a pattern and lose it - and NEVER EVEN KNOW IT. Track your progress. Okay, there's nothing better than an example to show you what I mean – and that's exactly what I'm going to provide to you right now.

This first example is a profile that I critiqued. My suggestions are in **bold**, and the original content is italicized:

Original Profile

"I'm just a young girl who wants to live a lavish lifestyle. I'm currently working my way up to Law School. I love being

spoiled at all times. I'm extremely active, I love going to sport-ing events, shopping and just having a good time."

Seeking in a Sugar Daddy:

"Looking for a Sugar who genuinely cares about me and my goals, a respectful Sugar Daddy who's willing to make sure that I am happy at all time. Willing to help pay for my col-lege tuition and pampering me in forms such as expensive gifts, travel trips and dates. I am not an escort." (If you are not an escort than you don't have to say it. Also the profile is NOT about you or your wants. It's about capturing the attention for them to respond that is the ONLY goal. Reread that.) *Please please help me out* (You come across as desperate).

Thank you in advance. (These words do nothing to add to your profile.)

What the Profile Should Say:

I have a confession to make: I'm having a torrid affair with running. There's nothing I love more than the overwhelming euphoria I feel after working up a sweat. I love how relaxed it makes my body feel…it's almost a seductive sensation that I just want to wrap myself in.

I can give you that same sensation. I want to make your pulse pound and your blood race as if you were running an ultra marathon. Won't you let me make you heart skip a beat?"

The Original Email Response

"Hi there, I'm Kelly. Your profile caught my eye and I was definitely interested in getting to know you a little better to see if we have any chemistry especially since we're both in the Miami area. Feel free to hit me up anytime. Muah." **(It comes across as a copy & paste – personalize with something directly on their profile not just because they are in the same area as you. Give them a reason to respond back.)**

What the Email Response Should Say:

"Hi there, I'm Kelly. Your profile really caught my eye, as I enjoy going for runs along Ocean Avenue as well. There's just something so thrilling about feeling the Miami sun beat down on your shoulders as you run to the sensuous music playing in the Cuban restaurants. Do you enjoy eating at any of these restaurants? I'd love to discuss our shared interests over a bottle of dark red wine."

I bet you can see the difference between the two profiles and two emails, can't you?

Throughout this book, I'll show you even more examples of statements and powerful words that will lure in generous and mature Sugar Daddies.

Let's Start From the Drawing Board

Pick four words that describe you. Now take those four words and describe them to something and use words that "evoke" an emotion. Also do this with three things you like or that interest you.

When you write you want your Sugar Daddy to visualize himself with you. He doesn't care what you do. He cares about how you will make him feel. So don't talk about yourself and what you want. We have the tendency to do that. Sugar Daddies are still men and unfortunately they don't often care about the little things.

So you have to appeal to their senses – and believe me, men are extremely visual. Now because they can't see you in person, your words have to stimulate them to feel something. Your goal isn't to attract many Sugar Daddies. Your goal is to attract the one that you want.

After all, quality is better than quantity.

Appeal to the Sugar Daddy you want. Now get inside his head. What would stimulate him?

Now talk to him with your words. You want to be descriptive so that they can relate in a stimulating manner.

Example: I love to "dance." This is how I would use

"dance" in my profile and the other words that describe "How it makes me feel":

> "I love to dance. It feels like nothing else and it's different each time. Sometimes it feels so freeing, like I'm flying, and it feels like pure bliss. Let me take you away. Escape with me to a place of serenity. Do you want to dance with me?"

As you can see through my example, you are still giving a little bit of you but your appealing to him. Men are visual creatures. You don't have to tell them a lot about you. Just give them enough to "want to get to know you."

Another Original Profile

Summary:

*In College, Looking for A Beneficial Companionship (**The headline can be better & stronger – this is your introduction – make them take notice otherwise you just get lost in the crowd. Think of this as going to the grocery store with a million of choices why should someone click on you. Be different.**)*

Description:

*Well hello there! (**This isn't necessary – think of every word in your profile matters and this is just wasted***

77

*space. Sugar Daddies don't spend a lot of time on pro-
files and you want to use your words to your advantage.)*
*I'm Jay, a college student with three minors. (**You don't have
to say it; instead, show it through your words. What are
you studying? Do you have a passion for your major?
Write something like that if you want to show your ed-
ucation**) I work out a lot with strenuous exercise. (**You don't
have to say it as it will reflect in your images**) I would
like a companionship that's mutually beneficial. (**You can just
take this out because it is not necessary.**) Very open-mind-
ed, curious (**Everyone says that...point out what are you
curious about**) If you'd like more pictures, please feel free to request them. (**Your goal is to find a Sugar Daddy, not give
them a portfolio.**) Can't wait to hear back from you. (**Your
ad leaves little to be desired when it comes to stimulating the mind. You are a fantasy to these men and you
should want to convey that.**)*

Description:

*Looking for a beneficial ....NSA keeps things fun. (**You want
to be more descriptive with what you are looking to
gain out of the relationship and you can do that by focusing on what qualities of the Sugar Daddy you are
after have and describe it in this section.**)*

Your Profile Should Seduce Sugar Daddies

Every word in your profile is powerful and you want
to choose your words carefully. The personal ad is not

about you. Reread that. It's all about your Sugar Daddy. Reread this again. You want to focus on what qualities that is unique to you so that your Sugar Daddy would be interested in you.

As a Sugar Baby you are a fantasy to these men. You want to build up that fantasy.

And it all starts with the profile.

What you want to do is tell a story with your personal ad and capture their attention to want to get to know you.

This is the start of seduction. This is your goal!

Now in order to make your ad better, you're going to have to be creative. You already have the ability within you. You just need to tap into it.

Example:

"I am your oasis away from the pressures of everyday life."

This sentence would appeal to a workaholic. Perhaps he is the CEO of a business and he is looking to escape from his typical mundane duties that are required of him. Although the personal ad is for him, you want to infuse it with a bit of you and why a Sugar Daddy would want to date you and jazz it up with your personality.

This starts with your goals because you're not writing the personal ad for every Sugar Daddy. You are writing it for the one that you want.

Example:

> "You will find yourself thinking of our last encounter and daydreaming of what sensual surprise I have in store for our next getaway."

This sentence gives off the idea she is not about routine and she would be exciting to be around.

You want to take your goals and the type of Sugar Daddy you are looking for and write to him specifically to draw him in.

Does this make sense?

For example, I play golf and not everybody plays, as it can be an expensive sport. I like going to cigar lounges and seeking out a cigar aficionado. I am a "foodie" at heart. I like to seek-out someone who has a passion for an ongoing love affair with finding a meal that is as unique and exquisite as me. I'm a businesswoman too and I like to surround myself with similar minds.

Now I can take those things that I am into and write it for the Sugar Daddy that I want - weeding out the ones that I am not looking for. For example, I can describe the feelings that I get when I unwind with a good cigar in a way that is yet sexy while titillating his senses to draw him in with the words that I use.

If you like the examples being used feel free to change them to make them your own.

More Examples

First, let's take a look at the bad personal ads. Read through these personal ads and see if you can figure out why these aren't going to be successful. Need some help? Not to worry, I'll walk us through why these Sugar Baby ads are bound to fail.

Describing Myself: Hello gentlemen, visiting MIAMI NOW, I'm originally from eastern Europe, beautiful blond, very loving and happy person, elegant and intelligent, great personality. Very slim, sexy, charming, love to be active, sun and the beach, travel and explore new places. I appreciate great restaurants, good wine and Champagne and I'm a very good cook! I live in downtown toronto (yorkville area), in my gorges penthouse with the best city views! I love sport cars, motorcycles, boating, walking on the beach, skiing, vacation in French Rivera or in the Caribbean, most of the outdoors activities or just quiet evenings by the fire. I preheat kindness in people and I would like to meet well established generous men who can be respectful and loving person, who can treat me like a princess and my job will be to make you happy! We can enjoy the finer things in life together, have fun and enjoy what life has to offer. I am looking to relax and enjoy life with men of similar interests. Email me soon, waiting for my Perfect sugardaddie / prince charming.

1. The first Sugar Baby ad immediately fails because it suggests that she's only in town for a short while. Additionally, the fact that she immediately capitalized "MIAMI NOW" makes me think that she's using a template profile, and she randomly inserts city names. In other words, I immediately suspect that this Sugar Baby is a fake.

Reading through the rest of the profile only confirms that, as she sounds like a description of what someone thinks a Sugar Baby looks and acts like. If this was a real Sugar Baby, her description suggests that she's already accustomed to the finer things in life, and she's only looking for a man to financially meet her expectations. To put it bluntly, she's just looking for a thick wallet, and probably won't emotionally invest in her Sugar Daddy.

> **Describing Myself:** I prefer to be called Sweets (a delicious nickname from my mom). I am from Richmond, VA and yes I do work just looking for some extra financial guidance. I'm a full-time mother (1 daughter) and student, very adventurous, out-spoken but a Lady! I'm thick in the hips and cute in the face. When I am not working or in school I enjoy listening to music, cooking, going to the beach (I love to feel the sand between my toes!) and doing adventurous things. Independence is important to me and I don't expect anyone to take care of me. Looking for a sexy sugardaddie, that is tall, dark and handsome. He also has to be successful, passionate about life, a gentlemen, adventurous and know how to treat a woman. If our relationship builds into something more that would be a plus. I would make beautiful piece of jewelry on any man's arm. I'm not for sale. But if you take care of me I will take care of you. If interested send me a message and we can take it from there and PLEASE have a picture posted.

2. The second Sugar Baby ad immediately makes me think that she's a prostitute ("Sweets"? Really?) Her interests are also pretty vague – I don't know anyone who doesn't enjoy music and cooking (or at least, eating). Describing herself as "thick in the hips" isn't exactly doing her any favors either; the word usage will immediately turn off mature Sugar Daddies looking for a classy and sophisticated lady.

Finally, her profile reads as a bit too defensive. Yes, it's important to be independent – but Sugar Daddies want to take care of you. Immediately broadcasting that you don't need a man to take care of you will make Sugar Daddies question why you're even on the site.

Describing Myself: My name is toya I just moved to Chicago I'm 21 I have no kids I love to dance and I love football I'm a huge steelers fan I'm starting school in January. I'm looking for somebody who can take care of me like I'm supposed to be tooken care of I'm not a boring person so you will enjoy your time with me. If you want to know more you can always send me a message.

3. Where to begin with the third Sugar Baby personal ad? First, her profile is riddled with spelling errors, grammatical mistakes and a host of other writing problems. If I were a Sugar Daddy reading this, I would immediately delete any of her emails – not only would they give me a headache trying to read them, but it suggests that she's of below-average intelligence who isn't serious about her search for a Sugar Daddy. At least, not serious enough to at least proof-read her profile (Sugar Daddies equate intelligence with social class). Finally, despite her protestations that she's "not a boring person," she sounds boring, as there are little personal details that make her sound unique.

Now for the good ones. Read through these personal ads and see why these girls will have their pick of Sugar Daddies. Now take a look at why I believe these personal ads to be the best ones out there:

Describing Myself: Hey! My name is Andrea I'm 21yrs old half cuban/brazilian and Israeli (odd mix I know) I live in Las Vegas where I finished and graduated from UNLV w/ a degree in Public Relations and on my way to get my masters. I also am a successful model having being published in many magazines from Maxim, Playboy, 944 and Glamour as well as print work for designers. I truly love it and want to take it as long as it can go! I'm a low key person and not much in the party scene although can party like a rockstar if I have too! I enjoy every oppurtunity and have a bit of a fiesty side, assertive and opinonated and whatever guy I get has to be masculine and can handle me! I am only looking for a Sugar daddie at the moment but open to letting life take its course but I would like to meet someone who is funny, charming, masculine and generous! I love traveling, working out, shopping and would love an arrangement as well. It has worked great in the past and hope I can find that ONE guy to have great memories with! I'm the best of both worlds wrapped in this feisty body! Hope to find the ONE soon! Xo. P.S. PLEASE DO NOT INSTANT MSG ME, If we click we can email or text (if we're compatible) Hope so! Muah.

1. You'd think that starting out these personal ads with mention of another Sugar Daddy would turn off potential suitors, but that's just not the case here. You see, Sugar Daddies love to see Sugar Babies who treat their Sugar Daddies with respect, enthusiasm and fondness, as they know that they'll be privy to the same feelings.

Describing Myself: I am very young at heart. Love being outdoors and listening to music that goes straight to the heart. Having dinner with friends. I believe in Karma especially what goes around comes around and live my life without judging others. Love to watch sports. Laughter really is the spice to life. I love to snuggle and have quite evenings at home. Looking for a Man who knows who he is, what he stands for. Someone who is strong and is as loyal to his mate as she would be to him. At this stage of my life I believe our best years are ahead of us. Kissing and touching is something I have to have in my life. I wake up the same every day! Thanking God, Loving Life and wanting a Man that does the same. I do not need a Man in my life, looking for a life partner. One that I can share my life with, someone who loves going to the gym, because he knows how important health and well being are. Someone who knows how important family and friends are. This is a beautiful quote to live by: To be rich in admiration and free from envy, to rejoice greatly in the good of others, to love with such generosity of heart that your love is still a dear possession in absence or unkindness - these are the gifts which money cannot buy. --Robert Louis Stevenson.

2. The second personal ad is also very warm and inviting, and you immediately get the sense that this Sugar Baby has a very strong idea of where she's headed in life. Her profile is highly engaging and pleasant to read, and she knows what she's looking for from her Sugar Daddy. Again, she makes no mention of finances, which means she's after a Sugar Daddy for more than his money. Finally, she's playful and shows that she loves to laugh, which is highly attractive to Sugar Daddies looking for a pleasant companion.

Describing Myself: If you are truly seeking a sugardaddie/sugarbabe relationship, I'm your girl (women is a better word). I know the role of a sugarbabe and I know what is expected from me. I do not play games and I am there to bring joy to your life, not add stress. Thanks to the help of a past sugardaddie, I currently own a small hair salon in Old Town Scottsdale that has been kicking my little ass around town. It's just a little over a year old and getting it established is one of the hardest jobs I've ever signed up for. A little about me. I'm as honest as they come (what you see is what you get), dependable, reliable and tons of fun. I've had too many obstacles in my life that I've overcome for the better, so I'm a survivor to the end. I'm just here looking for a little help with any bumps in the road that might be headed my way. Like I said, I know my role and know it well (love the role) and I'm not here to play games, so please give me the same respect in return. Everyone have fun in your search and may we all find what it is we desire.

3. Okay, so there are a few spelling errors in this last profile – but what it lacks in correctness, it more than makes up for in her sensual approach to Sugar Daddy relationships. Her profile reads seductively, as she highlights her want to be with a Sugar Daddy who is looking for a meaningful and highly satisfying relationship. For Sugar Daddies looking for a warm and loving companion, this is the perfect Sugar Baby for them. Yet again, there's no mention of money here, which means she's after a mature man for more than his bank account balance.

Create a Profile That Attracts the Right Sugar Daddy

The perfect personal ad to attract the right Sugar Daddy for you won't be a one-size-fits-all type of deal. Too many Sugar Babies make the mistake of doing that – and then they wonder why they end up on dates with Sugar Daddies who have different expectations.

No, if you want to attract the Sugar Daddy that's right for you, you need to assess exactly which type of Sugar

Daddy personality you're after. Not sure what these are? Not to worry – here's a quick review of the Sugar Daddy Personality Types:

1. The Mercenary Sugar Daddy. The mercenary Sugar Daddy falls into two subtypes: Old Money and New Money. A Sugar Daddy who is used to money (Old Money) and is bored by what it can get him; therefore, he expects more from his Sugar Baby than just looks. The New Money Sugar Daddy, on the other hand, is likely looking for a flashy Sugar Baby who's good in bed.

2. The Emotionally Starved Sugar Daddy. This Sugar Daddy is looking for an emotional connection. This Sugar Daddy wants a Sugar Baby who isn't just attractive, but has more traditional values as well. Trust is a huge factor for this type.

3. The Sugar Daddy Enhancer. This Sugar Daddy wants an attractive and articulate Sugar Baby who appreciates the same lifestyle that they can offer. With the right Sugar Baby on his arms, this Sugar Daddy wants to take advantage of everything that the world has to offer!

4. The Traditional Sugar Daddy. This Sugar Daddy may make a lot of money, but his values certainly haven't changed. He wants a Sugar Baby who wants to be cared for and loved, but not because he has plenty of money. His self-worth is on the line here – therefore, this type of Sugar Daddy needs a Sugar Baby whose motives aren't purely financial.

Now that you've familiarized yourself with the four types of Sugar Daddies, let's take a closer look at how you can create a personal ad that will attract your preferred type.

Catching Your Sugar Daddy's Eye with These Personal Ads

Have you determined which type of Sugar Daddy that you'd like to attract? Good – now you can easily write up the type of personal ad which will attract him the most. Use these tips and tricks below to get your Sugar Daddy to start emailing you before he's even finished reading your profile!

- If you want to attract a Mercenary Sugar Daddy, you need to highlight yourself according to his specific tastes. If you're after an Old Money Mercenary, talk about traditional aspects of yourself, like your goals for the future or your upbringing. If you're after New Money, then you need to highlight just how much fun you are, and how you can turn any gathering into the party of a lifetime.

- Want the Emotionally Starved Sugar Daddy? Talk about how you're a great listener, and all of your friends flock to you for advice. Remember, he's looking for an emotional connection here, so he wants to make sure that you'll establish one with him.

87

- If you're after the Sugar Daddy Enhancer, then be sure to mention that time you backpacked around Europe, or how you'll drop everything for an impulsive weekend trip to some far-flung corner of the continent. He's after a Sugar Baby who's just as adventurous as he is – so you need to prove that to him!

- Finally, if you want to catch the eye of the Traditional Sugar Daddy, combine the tips mentioned for the Emotionally Starved Sugar Daddy and the Old Money Mercenary. He wants an emotional connection with a Sugar Baby who oozes class, sophistication, and above all, discretion.

Crafting the Profile Worksheet

If you're not getting responses from your personal ad, this means it failed. Not the Sugar Daddies. Not the Sugar Daddy dating site. None of these failed. Your Sugar Baby profile crashed and burned.

If you are new to Sugar Daddy dating, use this worksheet to help with your foundation.

Let's Start from the Drawing Board

Think of words or phrases that describe who you are and some of the things you like. This may be more difficult than it sounds. If you have trouble thinking of things, concentrate on how you've spent your time over the last week. What hobbies have you pursued? Have you looked forward to watching particular shows or are you reading any interesting books? If you didn't have any responsibilities for the next week, how would you spend that time? Take the time to think about these things and write each item down.

Pick four words that describe you:
Example: (Considerate, Athletic, Adventurous, Entrepreneurial)
1.
2.
3.
4.

Pick three words that interest you:
Example: (Love Dancing, Cigars, Foodie)
1.
2.
3.

When you write you want your Sugar Daddy to visualize himself with you. He doesn't care what you do. He cares about how you will make him feel. So don't talk about yourself and what you want. We have the tendency to do that. Sugar Daddies are still men and unfortunately they don't care about the little things.

So you have to appeal to their senses.

Now take those four words and describe them to something and use words that "evoke" an emotion. Also do this with three things you like or that interest you.

Your Interest/ Descriptive Word	What makes you (Descriptive word that describes you)? How does your (Interest) makes you feel?
Example: (Love to Dance)	It feels like nothing else and it's different each time. Sometimes it feels so freeing, like I'm flying, and it feels like pure bliss.
Example: Cigar Aficionado	Smoking a cigar is like tasting a good wine: you smell it, you taste it, you look at it, you feel it - you can even hear it.
1.	
2.	
3.	
4.	
5.	
6.	
7.	

You should also take the time to assess yourself and determine how your own unique personality traits appeal to your Sugar Daddy. What is it about you that he'll absolutely find irresistible? How do your personality traits mesh with his? Understanding the main highlights of your personality can help you bring value to your Sugar Daddy's lifestyle.

"Always keep in mind that you should always be selling what makes you valuable."

Every Sugar Daddy has "hot buttons" – and only the most successful Sugar Babies are those that can ascertain what the other person's hot buttons are and then mirror their values to those needs and personality traits. Always keep one fact in mind: BEHAVIORS + FEATURES = VALUE. This is the secret to your "Sugar Baby Allure."

What is your Sugar Baby Allure?

Example: "I am an oasis away from the pressures of everyday life."

What do you bring to the relationship? (*Why Should a Sugar Daddy date you?*)

Write a one page informal document describing who you are, your strengths and your interests. Focus on the positive. Do not worry about grammar and editing. Simply put on paper "who you are" as if no one else were to read it. This will help make you more comfortable with writing about yourself, which will show in your writing.

Write a dating profile that gets results! Start with a unique introduction and try using effective techniques by including humor, posing a question or emphasizing a unique characteristic of your Sugar Baby Allure, or showing your sensuality.

Encourage potential Sugar Daddies to respond and learn more.

The 10-second Tip that Instantly Transforms Your Sugar Baby Profile

I have a writing tip so powerful, it'll transform your Sugar Baby Personal Ad instantly so it becomes more engaging, more persuasive and far more effective.

It'll make your head spin.

Ready? Do this:

1. Grab your profile.

2. Pick a sentence.

3. Change that sentence to "evoke" an "emotion."

That's it! **This is the secret.** You're writing directly, clearly and personally to your potential Sugar Daddy.

See for yourself:

I love to dance. I really enjoy meeting people (I am a people person), I like the theater and love a good dish.

Sounds pretty egotistical, no? Read what happens when I focus on "evoking" an "emotion":

"I love to dance. It feels like nothing else and it's different each time. Sometimes it feels so freeing, like I'm flying, and it feels like pure bliss. Let me take you away. Escape with me to a place of serenity. Do you want to dance with me?"

Big difference? Exactly.

10 Craft a Response That Draws Him In... And Puts It on "Auto Pilot"

Now that I've walked you through the process of creating a killer personal ad for your specific Sugar Daddy personality type, it's time to teach you yet another vital skill to capturing your Sugar Daddy...

...Crafting an intriguing email response that will leave him begging for more.

Of course, your email response will largely depend on the type of Sugar Daddy personality you're after, and what the Sugar Daddy has to say in his online profile. What you certainly don't want to do is just copy and paste a template response that will make your Sugar Daddy feel

turned off by your efforts (for example, I knew a Sugar Baby who had me generic introductory email that she sent to all Sugar Daddies – needless to say, she wasn't very successful).

So with this in mind, let's discuss how to craft dynamite responses based on the type of Sugar Daddy personality you're after:

Mercenary Sugar Daddies: I've said it before, and I'll say it again: these guys are absolutely defined by their money. However, this doesn't mean that you should send a response to their profile ad which talks exclusively about money; after all, they're quite protective of their wealth. If you're responding to an Old Money Mercenary ad, be sure to highlight your shared traditional values; if you're responding to a Money Mercenary, ask him if he's ever been to a big-name club in town.

Emotionally Starved Sugar Daddies: These Sugar Daddies want to make an emotional connection – so if you want to craft a dynamite response, you have to make the email all about them. After reading his profile, ask a follow-up question about one of his values or something else he mentioned. Don't ask about his line of work, as he won't want to establish an emotional connection on that basis.

Sugar Daddy Enhancers: These Sugar Daddies are adventurous, outgoing and impulsive, so a dynamite response needs to reflect your own abilities to keep up with him. Mention your own crazy travel adventures in your response, or simply talk about a time when you were incredibly impulsive. He'll be drawn to you like the proverbial flies to honey.

Traditional Sugar Daddies: If you want to craft a dynamite response to these Sugar Daddy types, then combine the advice from the Old Money Mercenary and the Emotionally Starved Sugar Daddy responses. He's a traditional man at heart, but he's still looking for an emotional connection with a Sugar Baby who will be sophisticated and discrete.

Now that you know how to create the kind of responses that will have Sugar Daddies knocking down your door, it's time to browse through your favorite online ads! This applies to all ads and responses use spell check and good grammar.

Creating the Sugar Baby Auto-Pilot System

You're a busy girl. You've got things to do. You've got people to meet. And although you want to put your all into Sugar Daddy dating, you don't exactly have the time to craft individual responses to all the interested emails you get.

And believe me, if you followed the steps from earlier courses, you'll be getting a lot of emails from interested Sugar Daddies!

But of course, you don't want to copy and paste auto-replies, because that will make Sugar Daddies lose interest. You want to find a way to respond to all your Sugar Daddies in less time, but still seduce them with your Sugar Baby story.

And that's where this autopilot system comes into play!

The autopilot system is exactly that: automatic emails and responses that you can send out to interested Sugar Daddies to let them know that you're interested as well.

Just customize the following responses below, and you'll have a stack of Sugar Daddy dates lined up before you know it!

Auto-Response #1

Hi here,

I've been looking for a connection like this for a long time with someone special just like you. Half of the thrill of this experience is feeling that head-over-heels stomach flip that means I'm either falling in love or falling in lust. I love the mystery of first encounters and

I love the electricity that sparks when you first touch someone that you're intrigued by. I'm not looking to be smothered, as this can make the spark die out – I am, however, looking for a relationship that stokes that spark into a burning fire. I want to find that with an older man, and I think we have the potential to experience a rich, exotic, and rewarding relationship.

I hope we both find exactly what we're looking for.

Auto-Response #2

You sound too good to be true. As a great conversationalist and intelligent, passionate woman, I've been looking for someone like you for a very long time. While I believe that half of the thrill lies in the search, there's no denying that I'm longing to feel that electricity that sparks when you first touch the person you share an undeniable chemistry with. Will we experience that spark when we first meet?

I'm not looking to be smothered, as this can make the spark die out – I am, however, looking for a relationship that stokes that spark into a burning fire. I want to find that with an older man, and I think we have the potential to experience a rich, exotic, and rewarding relationship.

I'm also interested in finding a man who not only shares my passion for passion, but also can be a mentor in my life. That's why I'm pleasantly aroused by the prospect of your profile, as you seem like a leader who can help shape my future.

I love the search as much as the discovery. Our compatibility will begin to be known by each of us on a much deeper level within minutes of meeting each other. Those first impressions will change moment by moment as our eyes meet and explore, as thoughts become words and are thus exchanged, and as we come to know each other's hopes and aspirations. After all, if you'll be my mentor you will need to know and understand all about past performance and future potential for growth and success.

The beautiful thing about what we have already begun is that we are very likely to become good friends at least, having met this way and explored each other without the usual restraints and reservations of meeting in more conventional ways. If we become torrid lovers as well, then we will be doubly blessed, because that is the most we should ever expect from a chance meeting. Either relationship could last a lifetime. I believe that either is worth the investment.

So if you want to go further, there's only one question remaining: what do we do next? I'm breathlessly anticipating your answer.

What if You Want to Reach Out First?

You put your time and effort into your profile. Once you're done, you sit back and wait for the Sugar Daddies to come swarming towards you. But a couple of days go by. Then a few weeks. By the time a month rolls around, you realize that you're missing out on quality Sugar Daddies...and you just don't know why.

So you become frustrated. Angry. Upset. You're losing patience fast – and you just can't figure out what to do.

Every Sugar Baby needs traffic and getting your profile clicked on is one of the most important steps you can take in getting your dream Sugar Daddy. You want a Sugar Daddy who is going to hunt down your profile and offer the world on a silver platter.

But here's something I want you to consider: you need to become a hunter as well.

Don't just let the Sugar Daddies come to you – instead, get out there and hunt down your dream Sugar Daddy.

Remember, the best Sugar Daddies strike a balance between being pursued and being the pursuer...

So if you see a Sugar Daddy you like, you shouldn't have to wait around for him to respond to you. Instead, take your destiny in your hands and reach out to him!

Of course, this doesn't mean you have to create a perfectly tailored response for every Sugar Daddy profile you come across. This can be time-consuming and troublesome, especially when you have a busy Sugar Daddy schedule you need to stick to.

That's why your emails to prospective Sugar Daddies should also be put on autopilot!

While you don't want to adhere to the "copy and paste" mistake (you know, when your email is so generic and vague that it's obvious you didn't read anything about the Sugar Daddy's profile), you do want to have a general template you can use to reach out to Sugar Daddies.

So take a look at these examples – and feel free to use many of them for yourself!

Email #1

Hi there,

I couldn't help but notice feel that we'd have a spark of electricity if we met. You seem passionate, exciting, and above all, filled with stories about [*insert something from the profile that he mentioned, like an interest or hobby]*. Our shared conversational skills could keep us entertained over a bottle of wine and a candlelit dinner for hours. There's nothing I love more than exchanging seductive glances with an intriguing and mysterious man like yourself while making intimate connections through our stories.

Now that I've introduced myself, I only have two questions remaining: Do you think the sparks would fly between us?

Are you willing to find out?

Email #2

There's nothing I love more than being pursued by an intriguing and powerful man — but there's something about your profile that's so compelling, I just had to take a chance and write to you. When you wrote that you (insert something from the profile that stuck out to you), I just could help myself from responding. I share the same passions and interests, and I felt like I was a moth being drawn to your flame. If you'd like, let's discover more about the sparks between us, and stoke that potential relationship into a bright and glowing fire.

So would you like to go further, the only question that remains is what next?

Put These Auto-Responders To Good Use!

Now that you have these personal yet automatic responses in hand, it's time to get as many Sugar Daddy dates as possible!

Listen: plenty of Sugar Babies are cautious about putting themselves out there. But don't let the fear of rejection prevent you from searching for the perfect Sugar Daddy. Time is money. Set up a schedule and send out ten to twenty messages each day and track your results.

Four-Step Process to Taking Your Sugar Daddy Relationship from Online to In-Person

You've been talking with your ideal Sugar Daddy for some time – and you're ready to move the relationship from the online world into the real one. But before you suggest meeting up in real life, take warning – many Sugar Babies often mess up this move by coming across as too forward, or waiting too long to meet up.

With that in mind, here is the four-step process to taking your Sugar Daddy relationship from online to in-person:

1. Setting up Your Personal Ad (The Hunter or The Hunted)

2. The Response to the Ad:

a. When a SD responds – Review his profile to see if you can find out more about his interests – they'll reveal a lot about your Sugar Daddy.

b. If he provides any personal information – like a phone number, name or his workplace - be sure to Google the information and see what you can learn.

c. The Direct approach – Responding to the ad (Hunter.)

3. The Reply

a. Building a connection – Talk about your common interests and ask him questions (just use the above template as a guideline!)

b. Setting expectations (Key to the Foundation of the Relationship) - Don't be aggressive or needy, as it comes across as being desperate. This process of setting expectations is a process that involves the both of you and must be completed before any serious Sugar Baby dating or sex happens.

4. Taking the Online Communication to the Next Step: Getting the First Date

a. When your SD asks you out – Don't accept right away, but do agree to his date within twelve hours after receiving the email. You want to seem in demand, but you don't want him to think that you're not interested.

If the Sugar Daddy says no to your request for a date, don't be rude. Instead, thank him for his time and wish him the best of luck. If he attempts to communicate with you despite denying your requests for a date, don't answer his emails.

If your Sugar Daddy agrees to go on a date with you, then congrats! I recommend that you head over to the *Sugar Daddy Formula* immediately and get your fill of tips, tricks and techniques you can use to make your Sugar Daddy fall head over heels for you on the first date.

However, be sure that you always follow this rule of thumb: absolutely NO sex on the first date. Don't become intimate with your Sugar Daddy until you've solidified your SB/SD relationship, including any financial details. It's just a way for the both of you to satisfy your own interests.

Creating the Sugar Baby Auto-Pilot System Worksheet

You don't want to copy and paste auto-replies, because that will make Sugar Daddies lose interest. You want to find a way to respond to all your Sugar Daddies in less time, but still seduce them with your Sugar Baby story.

And that's where this autopilot system comes into play!

The autopilot system is exactly that: automatic emails and responses that you can send out to interested Sugar Daddies to let them know that YOU'RE interested as well.

Just customize the following responses below, and you'll have a stack of Sugar Daddy dates lined up before you know it!

Just follow these three steps to create your own Sugar Baby Auto-Pilot System.

Three Step Process for Creating Your Own Sugar Baby Auto-Pilot System

- Step One: Build an Instant Connection

- Step Two: Introduce Yourself

- Step Three: The Call To Action

Step One: Build an Instant Connection

You want to start off with a compliment to these potential Sugar Daddies. Review his profile and follow that up with something that opens a connection to the potential Sugar Daddy you want to introduce yourself to or follow up from an email you received.

Example: *I've been looking for a connection like this for a long time with someone special just like you. But I hope you understand that I'm a bit hesitant about making that connection until I actually speak to you, and then meet you. It's just that there are so many rip-offs on the Internet that I need to protect my heart as much as possible.*

Example: *I couldn't help but notice that we'd have a spark of electricity if we met. You seem passionate, exciting, and above all, filled with stories about (insert something from the profile that he mentioned, like an interest or hobby).*

You want this short and to the point. To help you with the formulation of the "instant connection" Answer this question:

What are you looking for?

Step Two: Introduce Yourself

This is important. After you've built the connection, now is the time to introduce yourself and say why you are here but you only want to share things that will help these potential Sugar Daddies want to trust you.

Example: *Half of the thrill of this experience is feeling that head-over-heels stomach flip that means I'm either falling in love or falling in lust. I love the mystery of first encounters and I love the electricity that sparks when you first touch someone that you're intrigued by. I'm not looking to be smothered, as this can make the spark die out – I am, however, looking for a relationship that stokes that spark into a burning fire. I want to find that with an older man, and I think we have the potential to experience a rich, exotic, and rewarding relationship.*

Example: *Our shared conversational skills could keep us entertained over a bottle of wine and a candlelit dinner for hours. There's nothing I love more than exchanging seductive glances with an intriguing and mysterious man like yourself while making intimate connections through our stories.*

You want to answer: Why you are here?

Step Three: The Call to Action

You are asking for two calls to actions: The first call to action is about offering up something they're interested in, without just giving it to them, because you want them to ask for it & the second call to action is all about getting these potential Sugar Daddies to take it out of email.

Example: *So if you want to go further, there's only one question remaining: what do we do next? I'm breathlessly anticipating your answer.*

Example: *Now that I've introduced myself, I only have two questions remaining: Do you think the sparks would fly between us? Are you willing to find out?*

List three Possible Closing Calls to Action to get these potential Sugar Daddies to respond:

1.
2.
3.

Put These Auto-Responders to Good Use!

11 Choose the Right Site

Whether you're a college girl looking for someone to help with tuition or you're looking for a married Sugar Daddy who understands discretion, you want to select the Sugar Daddy dating websites that places you where your targets are.

And when combined with the techniques you discovered in the last two chapters, you'll be well on your way to finding the Sugar Daddy of your dreams.

Choosing a Site That Will Accelerate Your Sugar Baby Potential

When it comes to choosing the right Sugar Daddy dating website, you want to make sure you're looking for a site that puts you in close reach of your target Sugar Daddy.

Select a Sugar Daddy site that is on one of the first two pages when you search with key words: Sugar Daddy Dating Site, Date Rich Men, Wealthy Dating, Sugar Daddy Dating. These sites have the most exposure, which in turn has the most members.

To determine if the key word you are using ranks high amongst others searching using the same word. Use the Google Keyword Tool (https://adwords.google.com). It was initially created to be a research tool for prospective Google Adwords advertisers.

But smart Sugar Babies (*like you*) can take advantage of this free tool. You can see how well your keywords ranks; the higher the number the more exposure.

Having an idea of what you want will help you select the best Sugar Daddy Site.

Not all sites are created equal and if you are older and placing your personal ad on websites who market towards college women isn't going to work in your favor. You should go for a traditional Sugar Daddy dating site or a site geared toward wealthy dating, which will put you in a more appropriate playing field.

For the Advanced: You can find a Sugar Daddy without actually being on a Sugar Daddy dating site online. You can strategically place yourself where your ideal targets are.

Sugar Tip: Do you know that the average LinkedIn member earns around $100,000 per year?

Target your ideal Sugar Daddies and go where they are. LinkedIn is a place for Sugar Baby professionals.

That $100K is the average, but with the right network you just placed yourself near the target that you want to meet. CEOs, Executives, Owners etc. are all on there.

It's being strategic with your approach and targeting your ideal Sugar Daddy.

Sugar Dating sites are over- crowded but with the right plan and the right approach; you just opened doors to a world that was invisible before. You are connecting with potentials who would be ideal for you. Some of the best prospects are the ones that don't know that they are Sugar Daddies.

This is no different from a woman going to a bar in a high-end district "free-styling."

It only becomes risky depending on how the approach is handled but the rewards can be sweet.

You position yourself by seeking his advice. People enjoy telling others what to do. Allow your potential Sugar Daddy to tell you his by making it easy for him to do so. If you ask him for advice he will be gratified when asked to assist in helping you plan your career, provide business advice and so much more.

Make an offer to take him to lunch at a time convenient to him, in exchange for letting you rape his mind. Well, pick his brain but if you use "I would love to rape your mind." He will be at attention. It goes to show that if you are dealing with a professional man (or wanting to) you can find him on LinkedIn and other professional networks.

It's how you play the Sugar Daddy game to make it an advantage for you. Like I said before some of the best Sugar Daddies are the ones that don't know that they are and you are just being smart about surrounding yourself with ideal targets and that is Smart Sugar Baby marketing. You can also find them on meetup. com too. You are now targeting select Sugar Daddies based on their interests.

Sugar Baby Key Point: Go where your ideal targets are. Then once you do. Focus on your approach. The idea is to put yourself in reach of your target and from there work your magic to reel them in.

List Ten Websites that Interest You – and Why?

Sugar Daddy Dating Sites that Interest You	Why This Particular Site
Example: SugarDaddie.com	*Example: I am looking for a Traditional Sugar Daddy Relationship*
1.	
2.	
3.	
4.	
5.	
6.	
7.	
8.	
9.	
10.	

12 Your Pictures Tell a Story

When it comes to capturing the mind and heart of a potential Sugar Daddy, your profile picture can play a vital role. Your profile picture can either make you look like the classy and wonderful lady that you are – or it can make you look like you're one string of a bikini picture away from being considered an escort.

It sounds harsh, but it's true. When you pick your Sugar Baby profile picture, you want to make sure you have a reason for doing so. Your profile picture should add to your Sugar Baby story, not because it's the sexiest picture in your photographic arsenal.

So there's only one question remaining: How do you want your potential Sugar Daddy to view you?

To make this decision, you want to highlight the one emotion that you want to display to your Sugar Daddy.

Do you want to appear mysterious? Alluring? Charming? Highlight your main emotion, and then find a picture that accurately captures this emotion. Just like crafting your profile. You don't want to give everything there is to know about you away. You are building up the mystery to want them to get to know you more.

If you don't have a picture that does that, consider having some pictures taken of you professionally. If that is not in your budget place an ad on Craigslist.com or find a photography school and find a student that is willing to do it for little to nothing that will take a photo for you to capture the look you want to represent you.

You can also upload a photo of yourself doing something that you love. For example, you could show a photo of you rock-climbing, or taking a luxurious sip of wine at an outdoor winery. Sugar Daddies love enthusiastic and active Sugar Babies, which will draw these men to you.

And whatever you do, don't upload bikini photos and overly sexy modeling shots, no matter how slamming your body may be. This screams "escort" – and if you're looking for high-quality Sugar Daddies, that's not the kind of message you want to send.

How to Choose the Right Pictures

In a perfect world each part of your profile would be measured equally but unfortunately it isn't a perfect world. In the real world, your profile photos are the most important part of your profile. The rest of your profile is important but a great photo is the thing that gets your profile viewed and your emails answered better than any one other area.

If you are getting very few contacts or limited responses to the emails you send you probably want to start thinking about how good your dating profile photo is. Many people tell me that their dating profile photo is "fine" but *fine is the last thing you want!* A fine photo is one that will cause you to blend in with all the other fine photos!

The real problem with most photos used on online dating sites is that **everyone is doing the same thing.** They're either holding a camera out in front of themselves or using photos that were never intended to be used as a profile photo. Normally, these photos aren't bad at all...they just don't stand out. They are not the type of representation that convinces other singles that you are the person they should be dating.

A professionally taken photo, on the other hand, will make you stand out in the right way. If you are not getting many contacts or if you are not getting many responses to the emails I would recommend considering a service like that.

Even if you decide you don't want a professional photo taken at least take your profile photo seriously.

In online dating, fine photos aren't much better than bad photos.

I'm not going to lie here. You could have the best Sugar Baby profile in the world – but if your picture lets you down, then there's just no way you'll be attracting the quality Sugar Daddies you're after.

You may think that you need to post a picture that displays your assets at their finest, but that's missing the picture (no pun intended) entirely. Like I've said before, any Sugar Daddy can pick up a beautiful woman who happens to look good in a miniskirt. What you want to do is separate yourself from these dime-a-dozen women by emphasizing what makes you so special not just as a Sugar Baby, but as a personal in general.

Here are a few quick-fire hints and tips on how to choose the right photos for your personal ad:

1. Keep the sex at a minimum. Your Sugar Daddy is looking for a companion – not just an escort. If you're too out there with the sex, it gives off a hooker vibe. Not only is that a major turn-off for great Sugar Daddies, but it definitely attracts the wrong kind of attention. If you're uploading a photo that shows your cleavage, make sure that your arms are covered. In fact, try to keep cleavage shots out of your profile and emphasize another just-as-sexy part of your body, like your legs.

2. Post a photo that shows you doing something you love. For example, if you're an avid hiker, post a shot of you hiking the mountains at Yosemite; if you love running, post a picture of you in the middle of the NYC Marathon. The more your photo tells your Sugar Daddy about your personality, the more likely he'll be to click on your profile.

3. Whatever you do, do *not* post photos of you trying too hard to look sultry. You may think you look like a model, but you just end up looking high-maintenance or cheap to your Sugar Daddy. Instead, post a picture of you with a warm and genuine smile. You'll be surprised at how successful a "normal" picture can be at attracting Sugar Daddies. After all, listen to the advice of John, a Sugar Daddy: "If I wanted a hooker, I would not be looking for a Sugar Baby. Those type of ads tell me a lot, like I'm liable to be one of many men in her life, or she's mostly interested in the money. I generally skip over the too-sexy personals."

Sugar Baby Recap

While your Sugar Daddy is a wealthy and powerful man, he's still a man. Even though there's a financial element to your relationship with him, he still wants to find a classy and articulate Sugar Baby who will be the epitome of discretion. If your profile communicates that, then you'll have any Sugar Daddy eating out of the palm of your hand.

13 Create Killer Headlines

Crafting Your Sugar Baby Headline

How you write the headlines for your profile makes the difference between Sugar Daddies reading your personal ad...

Or ignoring it completely.

With this in mind, there's only one question remaining: are you using your headlines to lure in your Sugar Daddies?

The goal of the headline is to get clicked on - to read your profile.

The headline is the lead into your profile. Once your write your profile comeback and write your headline. Pick out something that standouts and then play with the arrangement of words to grab their attention.

Sugar Daddies don't have the time to read *every* profile. They jump from picture to headline. And they'll only move forward to read a profile if the headline or picture captures their interests.

Let's see how to write headlines correctly. Remember, they MUST capture the interest of Sugar Daddies if you want them to click through and read the rest of your profile.

Here are the fifteen types of attention-grabbing headlines with examples of each to help you understand how to use them more effectively:

1) The question headline: "Do You Want To Dance With Me?", "Can I be the Cigar to Your Lips?"

2) The command headline: "This is your chance to discover true seduction. Take it!"

3) The indirect headline: "A special reward is waiting for you at the finish line..."

4) The guarantee headline: "I guarantee I'll help you discover what it's like to be excited for life again!"

5) The frustration/problem headline: "If tomorrow was your last day, do you think you would have had enough fun?"

6) The personalized headline: "Finally, you've discovered the fun and sweet Sugar Baby you've been waiting for."

7) The benefit headline: "Clicking on my profile is guaranteed to make today instantly exciting."

8) The "Reason Why" headline: "Five reasons why you want me as your Sugar Baby."

9) The short but intriguing headline: "Sugar Daddy wanted now!"

10) The numbered headline: "The seven secrets I'll only reveal to my Sugar Daddy."

11) The "If... than" headline: "If you become my Sugar Daddy...You will wake up every day with a smile on your face!"

12) The invitation headline: "Let's go tear up the town together, shall we?"

13) The offer headline: "I'm exciting...intriguing...and you're just a click away from discovering why."

14) The "Facts You Should Know About" headline: "The Three Facts You Should Know About Me."

15) The combination headline: This is nothing more than mixing or combining of two or more of the headline techniques above. The end result of several combinations is a new version that has even more attention-getting and interest-arousing capability.

Great Keywords Make Great Headlines

When you're creating your headlines, every word counts. You want to choose words that communicate what you want in a way that is fast and impactful.

With that in mind, I'm going to share with you some of the keywords that I have found to be the most effective.

Words like "free," "sale," "exciting," and "last chance" all have the power to make people interested, excited and curious in whatever's attached to those words. Experts like to call them the "power keywords" – and if any business wants to be successful, then it's in their best interest to learn how to wield these mighty words.

Guess what? When it comes to Sugar Daddy dating, you've got your own set of power keywords – and if you learn how to use them, you'll have a stampede of Sugar Daddies knocking down your door!

- Exciting: Men love Sugar Babies with a zest for life – and if you mention that you find things in your life "exciting," "amazing" and "fantastic," he'll be instantly drawn to your positivity and enthusiasm for living.

- Focused: Although Sugar Daddies know that their relationships with Sugar Babies have a financial aspect to them, this doesn't mean they

128

want to fully support their Sugar Babies. That's why they're so attracted to Sugar Babies with their own career goals and interests. Talk about what you want from your future, and we guarantee he won't get enough of you!

- Tempting: On the other hand, it doesn't hurt to reveal your sensual side to your Sugar Daddy. Turn on the flirt and use power keywords like "tempting," "sensuous," and "revealing" to make his mind wander.

When it comes to creating hard-hitting headlines that attract and keep top-quality Sugar Daddies, never underestimate the power of your words!

Headlines for Every Sugar Daddy Type

Now that you have the pieces of great headlines, I'm going to put it all together for you right here.

When it comes to online Sugar Daddy dating, the title of your ad is everything. That's why you need to create an eye-catching profile title that doesn't just reveal a bit about yourself, but will also catch the eye of a generous Sugar Daddy.

Rather than making you do all of the work, I've compiled a list of titles that you can use for each Sugar Daddy type. Just customize them to fit your own needs.

Mercenary Sugar Daddies

Old Money –

- Sophisticated Woman Seeks Enlightened Man to Teach Her the Ways of the World.

- Well-Traveled Woman Wants a Man to Show Her the World She Has Yet to See.

- Eloquent Lady Desires a Man Who Can Prove that Talk Isn't Cheap.

New Money –

- See the City Lights Anew with a Woman Looking for a Good Time.

- This Spunky Woman will Rock your World from Dusk til Dawn.

- Never Be Bored Again! This Woman Is Ready to Really Let Loose.

- Life of the Party Looking for a Man that Can Keep Up.

Emotionally Starved Sugar Daddies

- Classy Woman Seeks a Deeper Connection with Her Man.

- Great Listener Looking for a Man with Plenty of Stories.

- Heartfelt Woman Seeks Man Looking for Love.

- Down-to-Earth Woman Ready for a Man to Hold Her Tight.

- Affectionate Woman Wants a Man to Share the Journey With.

- Loving Girl Seeks a Man who Knows the Importance of a Hug.

Sugar Daddy Enhancers

- Free-Spirited Girl Seeking to Embark on Enlightening Adventures with Her Man.

- Ambitious Woman Ready for New Experiences of All Kinds.

- Cultured Woman Seeks Man with an Eye for Art and an Taste for Fine Dining.

- Worldly Woman Looking to Travel and Learn with her Man.

- This Woman Wants to See the World and Experience it All.

<u>Traditional Sugar Daddies</u>

- Respectable Woman Seeks Man to Care for Her the Right Way.

- Upright and Honest Girl Looking for a Man who Shares Her Values.

- Classy Woman Desires Man with Something More to Offer.

- Sincere Woman Seeks a Man that Understands What Really Matters.

Use these headlines as a template, or come up with your own based on your ideal Sugar Daddy's personality type!

Headlines Worksheet

As you've learned, the headline is one of the most important parts of your personal ad besides your picture. It determines whether or not Sugar Daddies will read your personal ad.

You may have the best written personal ad in the world but you've wasted your time if your headline doesn't excite Sugar Daddies enough to read your message.

A SIMPLE FIVE-STEP PROCEDURE

I've used the following five-step procedure many times to create powerful headlines. It's simple and easy to follow. Even someone without special talent, skill or previous experience can use it to create a captivating headline.

STEP ONE

Define in writing the ideal Sugar Daddy you want to capture with your headline. Be sure to include the characteristics that make your Sugar Baby Allure irresistible to this potential Sugar Daddy.

> **Example:** *I'm looking to lure in my Potential Sugar Daddy by enticing him with my love of cigars in a seductive and tantalizing way.*

STEP TWO

Personalize this ideal Sugar Daddy by visualizing them as one person you want to attract with your headline. Keep this vision of one person in your mind whenever

133

you're writing a headline. Your personal ad will be read by one person at a time. Therefore, you'll find it easier to produce an effective headline by visualizing just one Sugar Daddy and writing to that person.

Example: I can envision my potential Sugar Daddy staring at my lips while the smoke is coming out of my mouth.

STEP THREE

Determine the most valuable benefit this potential Sugar Daddy will gain from your Sugar Baby Allure that is outlined in your personal Ad.

Example: He will see me as mysterious and want to know more.

STEP FOUR

Write as many one sentence statements as you can about your Sugar Baby Allure. Use one or more of the words from the following list in each statement. There are many other power words you can use in your headlines. However, many years of trial and error have taught me these five are the most effective:

Do you, Discover, You Should, Let Me, Want to, "X" with me,

Example: Let me be the cigar to your lips...
1.
2.
3.
4.
5.
6.
7.

8.
9.
10.

STEP FIVE

Select the most powerful statement on your list. If you have several that seem equally powerful, try making several ads to split tests.

That's it! You've just created a powerful headline to capture your potential Sugar Daddy's attention and provide a compelling reason to read your personal ad.

14 Test, Test, Test

I am a huge advocate of split testing your Sugar Baby personal ads. I believe that split testing leads to amazing results: Sometimes it is a simple as: Change one sentence = double your response rate.

Strategy + Schedule = Sugar Baby Success.

Today it's all about improving the results of your Sugar Baby profile. One of the best ways to improve your results is with split testing.

Testing is vital to your Sugar Baby success; it is a powerful strategy for increasing the effectiveness of your personal ads.

Split testing is also known as A/B testing. For the beginners out there, it is the process of taking one ad (your control or ad "A") and then creating another ad

137

(ad "B") – note you only make one change on the B version.

Then you track the results. One ad will get better results (usually and if it doesn't, you need to test something else, probably something more drastic). Once you have a winning ad that gets you the response rates you want, that becomes the new control to work with.

You create another version to test to see if you can improve on these results. With continual testing, you can improve your results and get more out of your personal ad and time you are spending to reach potential Sugar Daddies.

Why I Love Split Testing

I love split testing. It takes opinions and personal preferences and guesswork out of your Sugar Baby marketing. I also love it when testing proves me wrong (when I think something will win and it doesn't) – it's a great way to learn and it improves my results with Sugar Daddies.

Think about it. If I were to just go with what I had thought would win, I would be constantly getting lower results than I can now get with my new ad, which is already proven to get better results.

We just don't know how the Sugar Daddy market is going to respond and even with a seriously sensual Sugar

Baby profile, we just can't predict the response. With testing, we don't need to predict. We can accurately and scientifically determine what is going to work and improve our Sugar Baby results.

Think about it, you are running various personal ads from possibly different Sugar Daddy sites anyway. Why not get the most out of them and increase your response?

Here is a quick breakdown of how to split test:

Step One: Identify a certain aspects of your ad that you would like to test (picture, headline, or content in your profile.) Before you start testing out which one you would like to test first base it off of the responses you are receiving or getting. If you are receiving a lot of messages asking how much for an hour then chances are you want to look how you are coming across. Is it the picture you are using showing a lot and it doesn't match what your profile is saying. You can understand a lot based on how Sugar Daddies are responding to you. If your profile isn't getting any responses, then start with your picture and your headline.

Step Two: Create another variation of that ad (in order for an A/B test to be accurate you can only change one thing on the personal ad).

Step Three: Review the results and determine which ad was the winner. That ad is your new control page, and you can now create a new ad B to test something else. The idea is you keep testing and keep improving the results.

You can test anything, but here are some of the most common things to test:

- Picture vs. no picture.

- One Picture vs Two

- Setting an amount that you are seeking vs. leaving it open.

- Headline.

- Negative versus positive text (Ready To Fall In Love? – that's a positive approach. Sick Of Being Alone? – that's a negative approach).

- Different calls to action.

- Weird images (like you see on all those Facbook ads) or "normal" images.

- Smiling versus unsmiling pictures (yes, something that small can impact your results!).

- Ending your profile with a question vs. "message me now."

The list is endless and if you aren't currently split testing, I guarantee you aren't getting the maximum benefit out of your personal ad...

And you need to start!

Here Are Some Examples of Split Tests:

Version 1:

<u>Message me now!</u>

Now, let's say you click through rate (number of Sugar Daddies that click on your ad) is 4.2%. (Views vs. response) You are happy, because that's better than you've ever done before. What most Sugar Babies do is keep running with that personal ad. What we want you to remember to do is Split Test.

All that means is create a second version of your personal ad, to compete against your first version and see which one wins.

So, now look at version 2:

<u>Do you want to dance with me?</u>

Do you see the difference? Ending with a question guides Sugar Daddies into what you want them to do, and that is to respond.

So, let's look at the results.

Ad 1 – 4.2% click through rate

Ad 2 – 5.1% click through rate!

You just increased your response rate by 21.4%! No extra effort, simply changing one sentence and getting an improved response.

Why did more Sugar Daddies respond to "Do you want to dance with me?" than "Message me now!" We don't know, we may never know, but we also don't care. All we know is we now improved our response rate!

Now are we done? Not even close. Now we take ad 2, and create another ad to split test against ad 2. You can constantly test two ads against each other and incrementally increase your response rates from Sugar Daddies.

Here's an example of how you can change your headline.

Version One:

Seeking My Cigar Aficionado…is that you?

Version Two:

Let me be the Cigar to your Lips…

In version one, I posed my headline as a question; in version two, it was a statement.

Results: The statement won – by a small margin, but still a winner.

So you get the idea, nothing is too small to test. Look at your personal ad and try setting up a split test on those pages. Try to improve your results.

You should be split testing not only the ads but where you put you ads. Example: Sugar Daddy Dating Site vs. Craigslist, Non-Sugar Daddy Site vs/ Wealthy Men, Paid vs. Free, etc.

Never stop improving your Sugar Baby profile

Your photo is the most important part of your profile. However, this fact doesn't mean you should ignore the rest of the profile!

Also, just because you've been dating online for a few weeks does **not** mean that you shouldn't be revising your dating profile! I would recommend looking at your profile once a week to make sure it is reflecting you exactly how you want it to. I found that the more I dated the more I realized specifically what I was looking for in a Sugar Daddy. It was important that I updated my profile as I came to these realizations...and it should be important for you to do the same.

How to apply these techniques by using this Three-Step Formula to Landing Sugar Daddies:

Step 1: Discover Your Unique Sugar Baby Allure

When you are trying to find a Sugar Daddy, you've got to fill a need within your Sugar Daddy and you want to position yourself as the one that can provide it.

I know that sounds complicated, but it's not. All you've got to do is this:

First, You are not going to appeal to all Sugar Daddies. Reread that and reread that again. Not all Sugar Daddies will be subjective to your charm and that is okay. You are not going to attract every single Sugar Daddy and that is ok. Figure out what makes you unique and why a Sugar Daddy would want to be with you.

Second, Write those unique qualities about you on a piece of paper, and then begin to write in a way to attract the Sugar Daddy you want.

And that unique allure is all that matters.

To be a successful Sugar Baby, you don't need to look like a super model. You need a unique Sugar Baby Allure.

Nothing works better than a real-life example, so here's mine:

I decided I wanted to find a Sugar Daddy that could be marriage material. He had to have owned a business, no kids, travels and had to be financially well off to provide for me and also had a disposable income in which he can also assist in my own business endeavors.

So what did I plan on doing to find him?

Instead of just writing a profile I specifically wrote for the Sugar Daddy I wanted. Instead of me describing the type of Sugar Daddy I wanted from the above I wrote my profile to stimulate his mind to draw him in. I began attracting higher caliber of Sugar Daddies. But having a unique allure wasn't enough...

Yes, when you're using the "find a Sugar Daddy" formula, having a unique allure is vital, but you also need something more.

And that's where this next section comes into play.

Step 2: How to Build Anticipation the Right Way

Why focus on building anticipation?

1. **Anticipation builds desire.**

2. Anticipation gets Sugar Daddies to respond.

3. Anticipation opens what's known as an information gap, and people can't wait to fill it.

How Do You Build That Anticipation?

You tell Sugar Daddies what they want to hear, but you're not too specific about it. You give details, but hold back the full details.

For example, when I put up a profile I would do it in a way that not only stimulated the minds of these potential Sugar Daddies but they were responding. I positioned myself as a never-ending book that they wanted to learn more.

Within the profile I controlled what emotions I wanted the Potential Sugar Daddy to feel and "evoke an emotion" within him and guided him on what to do next.

And what happened? Sugar Daddies were responding.

The reality is this: Most Sugar Daddies aren't going to read your profile. You want to grab their attention with your headline and say more with fewer words to build that anticipation. You get two chances to grab attention instead of one: Headline and the content in your profile.

Anticipation works.

Step 3: How to Deliver

Here's where things get sticky...

When you build anticipation, you've got to deliver. I know that sounds simple, but I've found that when people just do what they say they're going to do, they're light years ahead of everyone else. This is also how you build Trust with your Sugar Daddy.

Now if you really want to woo your potential Sugar Daddies... and ensure that these Sugar Daddies *know* you brought the goods... you should over deliver.

Here's how:

1. The reply from when he responds to your ad – For example, after you write your ad it doesn't stop. You are a never ending book and that continues. Continue your Sugar Baby Allure from your profile to the replies that you will send back to these potential Sugar Daddies. You want to keep the image you want to have with them and continue to guide them. This is the perfect place to gather information from your Sugar Daddy by asking him what he is missing and things that interest him. The key here is to get to know him and understand him and build trust. You also want to qualify your Sugar Daddy. Can he afford you?

2. Trust – Taking it offline and meeting. Your first meeting is essential for building trust.

3. Deliver – You can't get around this. No matter what allure that you used to reel in your potential Sugar Daddy, you've got to make sure you're delivering what it is that they want but in the same time getting what you want.

And that's it.

Part Three:
You Can *Always Get What You Want*

R emember the old Rolling Stones song, "You Can't Always Get What You Want?" Well, you can – and with the right Sugar Baby marketing, you will!

I'm convinced that many Sugar Babies have a hard time with their Sugar Baby marketing because of their unwillingness and resistance to being where they are right now. They say:

"I don't know where to start. I want to be somewhere else. And I want to be there as soon as possible!"

"I want to have a perfect Sugar Daddy."

"I want an allowance, and shopping sprees."

"I want a profile that attracts the Sugar Daddy I want."

"I want to be able to negotiate with my potential Sugar Daddies about the relationship so that I get what I want."

149

"I want to know how to ask my Sugar Daddies for what I want."

"I want $1,000-$3,000 every month, now!"

Sure, at one level, there is nothing wrong with these. It's a great thing to have goals and go for them. And from one perspective, these are great Sugar Baby Marketing goals.

But because they're not yet a reality, we are frustrated, anxious, and worried about the future, thinking we'll never get there. So instead of using goals as beacons to move forward, they become a burden, reminding us that we're not there yet.

And since things aren't perfect, we put ourselves and our Sugar Daddy Dating on hold until we get everything into place. It's kind of like the Sugar Baby who needs to lose twenty pounds before she starts dating. And of course, only when she's bought the perfect wardrobe and gotten a makeover, will she be ready for dating.

You know how that works out!

I see this tendency with Sugar Babies all the time: "Well, when I have my perfect body I'll get out there." And I say, "Well, why don't you get out there and try it out now? And then as you lose it you can fine-tune your approach with finding the one you want." And then they say, "Well, I'm not ready yet, give me a few more weeks to get it right!"

Hopeless, right? You don't need to get ready to get into the NOW. It's 100% here, right... NOW!

So the first things to remember about goals, is first you need to be perfectly OK about exactly where you are right now. In this moment, there is nothing you need to change. Be OK with your current situation as a Sugar Baby. After all, it's what you have to work with right now.

And then you take the first step. You put up your profile on a Sugar Daddy Dating site and start responding to Sugar Daddies. You look at the results you are getting. No results. Then you take a look at how you are coming across. Do you see how perfect that is?

Now you have some data to work with!

You try a different profile and or/message with the next go around. They are mildly interested, but the conversation doesn't really go anywhere.

Perfect again. And you're getting the hang of it.

In every step of the process you were exactly where you needed to be. You were not focused on being a "perfect Sugar Baby" where you sashayed onto a Sugar Daddy Dating site with 100% confidence and connected

151

with every Sugar Daddy who reached out to you, talking with ten solid potential Sugar Daddies.

That's a fantasy, by the way.

Sure, you might aspire to that, but now that you've set your goals, take your mind off of them, and especially off how you think you should be as far as your Sugar Baby marketing skills and results go by focusing on where other Sugar Babies are in their journey, and just focus on the NOW.

This goes for everything in your Sugar Baby marketing: Your profile, your target Sugar Daddy, your Sugar Baby Allure, your conversations, and how you market yourself as a Sugar Baby.

There's one thing for certain for every Sugar Baby reading this: All of those things in your Sugar Baby marketing are exactly where they should be right now. You have the skills you have right now; you have access to Sugar Daddy Dating sites right now; and you're exactly who you are right now.

Perfect. How could anything possibly be missing?

And that's the only place you can work from. And from that place of NOW, you can produce Sugar Baby miracles.

I Hate Writing – So How Do I Make Online Sugar Daddy Dating Work?

I know for many of you writing can be awful, but writing is so crucial to capturing the attention of your dream Sugar Daddy. Your words are an extension of you – and they need to show your Sugar Daddy that you're interesting, exciting, and absolutely intriguing.

Intimidating, isn't it?

I know you're expecting me to say to practice writing your profile out until it sounds pitch perfect.

But guess what? **If you hate writing – don't do it.**

"Taylor's 80/20 Rule" says spend all your time doing those "20% things" that bring you "80% of your returns". If writing is not one of those things for you, then hire somebody else to do it and get back to doing what you do best.

So why not have a professional take care of this really important thing for you? Check out the Sugar Profile Writers (writing service that makes your Sugar Baby profile standout) at TheSugarDaddyFormula.com.

15 The Biggest Mistakes Wannabe Sugar Babies Make

Hey, we're only human – and that means we all make mistakes.

But when it comes to dating your Sugar Daddy, your mistakes need to be few and far between. After all, these wealthy and powerful men are inundated with offers from beautiful and intelligent women from around the world – and if you want to stay on his mind, then you need to avoid the three classic mistakes many Sugar Babies make with their Sugar Daddies!

Classic Mistake #1. You don't properly manage your expectations. Guess what: if your expectations are too high or too low, your Sugar Daddy is bound to lose interest in you. If your expectations are too high, don't demand the world from him. Instead, compile a basic budget in mind and approach him with it on your second date. Don't play the numbers down either: if you want that tuition bill paid or you expect a few shopping trips here and there, then let him know about it.

Classic Mistake #2. You gave in to his sexual demands too quickly. Yes, sex is a part of the Sugar Daddy relationship – but that doesn't mean that you need to give into his physical urges right away. Hold off on the sex until your Sugar Daddy proves that he's as good as his word. That way, you can fully give yourself to him without any of those nagging doubts!

Classic Mistake #3. You're a negative person. Heck, we all like to think that we're positive people. But if you have a tendency to complain or gossip too much, then don't be surprised if your Sugar Daddy bids you good-bye. Sugar Daddies love being around happy and positive women – so smile and show your appreciation for life!

If you can avoid these three common mistakes with your Sugar Daddy, then you're guaranteed to have a very successful relationship!

And These 6 Other Mistakes...

You thought you and your Sugar Daddy had a great time on that date last Friday, but apparently he thought otherwise. After texting, emailing and calling his phone to no avail, you're ready to admit defeat yet again. It seems like no matter what you do, you just can't get a good guy to stick.

So are you just a magnet for back luck – or are you committing one of these six common mistakes with your Sugar Daddies?

1. You had *too high* expectations. Even the wealthiest Sugar Daddies don't like feeling as though they have to live up to your sky-high financial expectations.

2. You didn't have *enough* expectations. Don't let your Sugar Daddy get away with an odd gift here and there; if you want more, then tell him.

3. You gave in to sex too quickly. There are some "Sugar Daddies" who will treat you like an escort if you let them.

4. You were too glum. People are attracted to those with a zest for life – so show those pearly whites if you want to keep your Sugar Daddies around!

5. You were too needy. Wealthy and powerful men like your Sugar Daddy are extremely busy; after all, it just

goes with the territory. Try to be more understanding of his schedule – he'll appreciate your patience.

6. And finally, you didn't give enough in return. Even the wealthiest Sugar Daddy won't want to spend time with a woman who expects everything for nothing in return. He's making an investment in your time and company – so make sure it's worth his while by being witty, charming and above all, fun!

The One Thing You Must Never Ask a Sugar Daddy ... Unless You Want to Scare Him Away

Your Sugar Daddy may be a wealthy and powerful man, but if you want to keep him around, then you need to understand that he can get easily concerned.

We're not talking about fears of flying, or his fear of heights. No, when it comes to your relationship with your Sugar Daddy, there's only thing that scares him: asking him one of these two questions!

"How Much Can You Afford?" This might seem like an innocent enough question. After all, how else can you determine if your Sugar Daddy will be able to meet your financial needs?

But by asking this question, you're essentially telling your Sugar Daddy that you have no idea what *you're* worth – and that's a recipe for disaster. You see, your Sugar Daddy wants to be with a Sugar Baby who knows exactly what she wants and isn't afraid to get it. As soon as you leave your worth up to him, you'll be devalued in his eyes. So approach him with a predetermined budget in mind – he'll see you as a woman who knows her business!

Wannabe Sugars vs. Real Sugar Babies

Twelve differences between those who dream and those who act:

1. Wannabe Sugars obsess about dilemmas. Sugar Babies obsess about action.

2. Wannabe Sugars want more traffic to their profiles. Sugar Babies focus on Sugar Daddy conversion.

3. Wannabe Sugars focus on hoping things will improve. Sugar Babies plan for multiple contingencies.

4. Wannabe Sugars want to get instant monetary support. Sugar Babies build their empire.

5. Wannabe Sugars seek a perfect profile. Sugar Babies execute and adjust the profile by always improving it.

6. Wannabe Sugars wait for their Sugar Daddy to find them. Sugar Babies engineer four, five, six strategies and execute them in tandem, certain that at least one plan will get traction.

7. Wannabe Sugars fear looking like a Gold-Digger or Escort and don't ask for what they want. Sugar Babies willingly risk and ask for what they want; knowing that long-term success is a good trade for short-term loss of dignity on how one will perceive them.

8. Wannabe Sugars shield their precious life goals from their Sugar Daddies because they want this lifestyle not to interfere with their personal life. Sugar Babies expose their ideas and goals to their Sugar Daddies to reach their goals faster.

9. Wannabe Sugars spend hours bashing other Sugar Babies with other Sugars about this lifestyle. Sugar Babies practice and improve their Sugar Baby game.

10. Wannabe Sugars believe what they're told, believe their own assumptions. Sugar Babies do original research and determine what paths have been already trod to success.

11. Wannabe Sugars believe they can attract any wealthy Sugar Daddy they want and get what

they desire. Sugar Babies focus on their Sugar Baby Allure to capture the interest of their target Sugar Daddy to increase their success rate to get what they are seeking.

12. Wannabe Sugars think about this lifestyle in terms of COULD and SHOULD. Sugar Babies think in terms of IS and CAN BE.

16 What He Wants

For many people, the term "Sugar Daddy" is inextricably linked with sex. To them, the Sugar Daddy/Sugar Baby relationship is one that's set up by an older and wealthier man who wants nothing more than a beautiful plaything for weekend nights.

However, those are the same people who can't understand what really goes on in the Sugar Daddy/Sugar Baby relationship. After all, if all a Sugar Daddy wanted was sex, then he could simply pick up his telephone and call his local escort service.

So why do Sugar Daddies pursue relationships with Sugar Babies? The answer's simple: because they're human – and they're looking for an emotional connection. They also view escorts as call girls and a Sugar Baby as more like a friend.

Many Sugar Daddies simply don't have the time or energy to devote to dating. And for those Sugar Daddies who are in relationships, the desire to seek another emotional connection outside of the marriage prompts many of these men to seek out intelligent, gifted and thoughtful women. It's not all about sex.

It's about the human desire to connect with someone who understands them on so many more levels than the physical one.

Understanding this need is crucial for any successful Sugar Baby. Your Sugar Daddy doesn't want just another fling or pretty thing – after all, as a powerful and wealthy man, he's probably inundated with these offers on a daily basis. Rather, it's important to understand that your Sugar Daddy craves companionship – and nine times out of ten, it has nothing to do with sex or physical intimacy whatsoever. What he wants most is your ATTENTION!

Remember, you can mix sex and companionship to ensure your Sugar Daddy will know you care. After you have had sex do not jump up for the shower. Take your queue from your Sugar Daddy – stay right where you are and rub his back or arm and talk to him. It almost don't matter what you talk about — just connect.

So if someone doesn't understand your relationship with your Sugar Daddy, just give them your best smile – because unlike them, you're lucky enough to have a Sugar Daddy who values your time, opinions and companionship!

Remember Your Sugar Daddy Types

I cannot say enough that every Sugar Daddy is different. Let's go over the four types of Sugar Daddies once again…

1. The Mercenary Sugar Daddy. The mercenary Sugar Daddy falls into two subtypes: Old Money and New Money. A Sugar Daddy that is used to money (Old Money) but is bored by what it can get him; therefore, he expects more from his Sugar Baby than just looks. The New Money Sugar Daddy, on the other hand, is likely looking for a flashy Sugar Baby who's good in bed.

2. The Emotionally Starved Sugar Daddy. This Sugar Daddy is looking for an emotional connection. This Sugar Daddy wants a Sugar Baby who isn't just attractive, but has more traditional values as well. This Sugar Daddy is all about *trust*!

3. The Sugar Daddy Enhancer. This Sugar Daddy wants an attractive and articulate Sugar Baby who appreciates the same lifestyle that they can offer. With the right Sugar Baby on his arms, this Sugar Daddy wants to take advantage of

everything that the world has to offer- he wants a big slice of pie with ice cream too!

4. The Traditional Sugar Daddy. This Sugar Daddy may make a lot of money, but his values certainly haven't changed. He wants a Sugar Baby who wants to be cared for and loved, but not because he has plenty of money. His self-worth is on the line here – therefore, this type of Sugar Daddy needs a Sugar Baby who never, ever makes him feel like her motives are just about money.

Now we're going to see some examples of how you can read the messages potential Sugar Daddies send you and determine what "type" of Sugar Daddy you're dealing with…

Message from Sugar Daddy #1:

Can't tell you what a pleasure it is to read your ad. No noticeable grammatical or spelling errors. Well worded, obviously written by someone intelligent, & apparently goal oriented, knows what she wants, & goes out to get it.

Did want to commend you on not asking for a bank truck full of financial assistance that you may wish to receive. I've read many (& never responded) to those that think that right off the bat, a man would be willing to part with copious amounts of cash for a start up relationship. Most have no idea that the sugar babes that have been most successful, never started out with such high ideals. Either that, or they kept the ideals a secret. When a man begins to care for a woman, as a lover, friend, confidante, he wants to please her. That's when he will willingly start to spoil her to a manner that she might want to become accustomed to. So, kudos on being smart enough to be aware of the best way to approach this matter.

Though I know you don't emphasis pics in your reply, I've chosen to send you some. This is done to save us time, if you find that I would not be attractive enough for you to consider, we should be aware of it asap...

So if I'm still of interest to you... Would like to arrange a lunch/coffee/trip to Paris meeting next week or two. If interested,, please send an email, or if you trust me enough, your phone number. I find it easier & more accurate to converse on the phone rather than emails. If replying, would like to know your name. Would really feel awkward, yelling "Hey you..." when I would try to garner your attention.. Hope you have a lovely day & am looking forward to hearing from you.

What This Tells Me About Him:

This Sugar Daddy certainly cuts to the chase, which tells me that he's experienced at Sugar Daddy dating. The fact that he complimented me so often during the email also tells me that he's eager to please – and the hints that he's had less-than-stellar experiences with other Sugar Babies tells me that he's an emotionally starved Sugar Daddy.

Message from Sugar Daddy #2:

How's the weeding out going? I believe we are on the same wavelength. I'm a finance professional who has done very well for himself. The problem is that it is for "himself" because I don't have a family yet and not currently in a relationship.

I've also been fascinated with the older/younger friendship scenario and believe I'd make a great "Life Mentor" for the right person. I'm not really interested in the "sugardaddy" role since that implies just an exchange of financial favors for sexual favors. I'm more interested in what I would call an "affectionate friendship" whereby we would be able to share our deepest thoughts and feelings, make each other laugh, create some imaginative adventures and each of us would grow into being a better and insightful person.

I guess the wording that appeals the most to me would be that I would like to be a "wise and trusting teacher" to someone. And since I'm financially secure that would also mean that I could make sure they have what they need as well as opportunities for fun life experiences.

Let me know what you're thinking. Hope to hear from you.

What this tells me about him…

This is definitely a traditional Sugar Daddy who is intellectual and looking to share with his opinions with a companion who's on par with his intellect. He wants to get married and have kids at some point, but for now, he's lonely yet financially stable.

His 2nd Email to Me (This was sent after I used the second of the two auto replies you'll soon discover)

Hi,

I really like the fact that you enjoy expressing yourself. It's like pulling teeth to get most to even write a sentence or two. Do you happen to have an interest in writing?

I guess next is we either arrange to meet or continue to exchange emails. Would you like to get a coffee, have lunch or dinner sometime? Did you have an idea on how you would like to meet?

You mentioned your interests. What are some of your favorite things to do?

What This Tells Me About Him:

This Sugar Daddy likes to communicate and is very considerate, and would be concerned more about my happiness then his own.

Message from Sugar Daddy #3:

I think I am impressed. There are two groups of (serious) men who would respond to your ad. One that is in a committed relationship & one that is single like me and free as a bird. Which one are you looking for searching for a long time she says?

Ate breakfast, read the sports pages, yes the old fashion way, played with the dogs, I just cleaned my kitchen, as I am peculiar about my kitchen while thinking of you.

I am a Gemini (just had birthday) 5'9" at 203 lbs. Izzy & Rascal (dogs) are my best buds, but I am blessed with a great group of friends who are all married except for one outcast. I have a Partner in my business, 5 employees, and just completed a project that needed an additional Thirty men. Mostly strong backs. I am a leader, loyal, honest, with plenty of free time. And fun. Garlic, olive oil (extra virgin) and chicken stock are some of the gifts from the Gods (plus hops, tequila, wine, & a nice roaring fire in the winter). Chicago is my favorite city, like to travel to warm weather beaches, and surprise my woman.

I love to mentor, share my experiences, and lead by example. I would enjoy the challenge of stroking your ego, stimulating your mind, and pleasing your body and senses while supporting you $$.

I look forward to tomorrow because you never know what lies ahead & it is only getting better. I am dabbling in the pleasures of a new car, new washing machine and new iPhone.

I am not looking to settle down, need my alone time, enjoy my freedom, but do not desire the coldness of NSA fun. I could go on and on but enough is enough.

I am interested.

<u>What This Tells Me About Him:</u>

He's a traditional Sugar Daddy who is well-traveled; he's most likely a businessman who considers his dogs to be his children. He's generous and giving, and is looking for a woman to bring whom he can bring around his friends and social gathering. He likely has a sense of humor, likes to cook and drink, and is looking to have someone around for a bit of excitement as his reply indicates that he's somewhat stuck in a routine.

What Every Sugar Baby Should Know About Sugar Daddies

Quick: what's the one thing that every Sugar Daddy has in common?

Is it that they're all wealthy and powerful men? Are they all attracted to beautiful young women with brains? Or is it that they're simply at a point in their lives where they're looking for a little fun outside of the home?

These are all good guesses, but guess what - they all fall short of the mark.

If you want to become a successful Sugar Baby, then you need to look beyond the obvious and the simple exterior of your Sugar Daddy. Sure, he may seem like the world is at his feet – but what's going on inside of him? Why has he specifically sought you out as a Sugar Baby? What is it about you that he just can't get enough of?

Believe me, it has very little to do with sex. After all, if your Sugar Daddy was just after sex, wouldn't it have made more sense to hire an escort than pursue a Sugar Baby? In fact, when Sugar Daddies are asked what their prime motives are for pursuing relationships with Sugar Babies, they all say the same thing:

It's about the emotional connection.

Your Sugar Daddy may be an important man, but this doesn't mean that he's not lonely. Perhaps the spark has fizzled out of his marriage, or he doesn't have enough time to develop a meaningful social life. You are his emotional connection in a world of business contacts and old lovers – and that's what makes you so important to your Sugar Daddy.

Two Early Warning Signs of a Fake Sugar Daddy

You just met your new Sugar Daddy, and he seems like the real deal. He's kind, courteous and he's not shy about footing the bill for your extravagant date. Yes, everything seems to be going well...

But that still doesn't explain why you can't shake the feeling that something's off about him.

As a Sugar Baby, your greatest weapon in rooting out fake Sugar Daddies is your intuition. If something seems off about a potential Sugar Daddy, then you should put on the brakes before letting the relationship progress any further. And if he demonstrates either one of these two early warning signs, then get out of that situation as quickly as possible:

1. He Insists on Becoming Intimate too Quickly. A true Sugar Daddy won't push to become intimate right away, meaning "right when you meet him." If your potential Sugar Daddy is trying to get you into the bedroom as quickly as possible, walk away – he's not a true Sugar Daddy.

2. He Refuses to Talk About Money. Talking about money is considered a social faux pas, right? Not when it comes to the Sugar Daddy/Sugar Baby relationship – in fact, you're expected to talk about financial matters! If you bring up money matters (for example, you want to talk about his contribution to the relationship) and he refuses to talk about specifics, then chances are you've got a fake Sugar Daddy on your hands depending on his Sugar Daddy type.

17 Ask for What You Want

Why Some Sugar Babies are Successful at Getting What They Want from Their Sugar Daddies

Some Sugar Babies seem to have all of the luck, don't they?

They're always decked out in the latest fashions. All of their bills are paid right on time. And it seems like they're off to visit some exotic location every other weekend with their incredibly wealthy and powerful Sugar Daddies.

It can be pretty tough to see this when you're not the Sugar Baby who's experiencing it. So does this all boil down to blind luck?

Or is there another reason why these Sugar Babies can get exactly what they want out of their Sugar Daddies?

Listen up, Sugar Babies: the reason why these girls are so successful is because they know exactly what they want from their Sugar Daddies in the first place – and they're not afraid to ask for it. Plenty of Sugar Babies enter the relationship with no expectations; instead, they simply expect the man to take the lead and offer to buy presents and pay for bills.

But without a predetermined budget, you can bet your bottom dollar that your Sugar Daddy will try to get away with the bare minimum – and you'll be left wondering how it all went wrong.

Of course, the key to success is in *how* you ask your Sugar Daddy for the things you want.

Simply put, you can't expect endless gifts unless you know how to time the question. Don't expect fabulous jewelry just for showing up for a date; instead, show your Sugar Daddy just what makes you so priceless as a Sugar Baby. Is it your smile? Your wit? Your ability to make anyone feel comfortable?

Work these features to your advantage, and you'll be flooded with gifts and money in no time at all!

Excuses, Excuses...

When was the last time someone said you are what you are worth?

If you are having trouble getting what you want from your Sugar Daddy, you may need help being able to negotiate for what you want. But first, you have to identify how much you're worth, and how much you're willing to ask for.

As a Sugar Baby, it's your responsibility to invest in yourself. We all know the reasons why you want to ask for a higher allowance: you need the money, you need an enhanced lifestyle, you want to be better off than you were before, etc.

So why do so few Sugar Babies actually ask for what they want?

I've identified the three lamest excuses why we don't ask and the techniques you can use to overcome them.

Number One Lame Excuse: Fear

Many Sugar Babies claim that it's too risky to ask for what they want, or they fear getting rejected by their Sugar Daddies. To which I have one thing to say: if it feels risky, then you're doing it wrong. You CAN get your Sugar Daddy to agree to give you what you want.

To do this, sit down with your Sugar Daddy to discuss the relationship before you enter into a relationship. Use these two key scripts to start the conversation:

Key 1. "What would it take for me to be [insert goal]?"

Just being a Sugar Baby isn't going to get you what you want. Instead, you need to appeal to your Sugar Daddy's desire to help you. For example, if you want to start your own business, ask his advice about how to start your own business. Your Sugar Daddy will love coming to your aid, and the offer for financial help will inevitably follow.

Key 2. "After I do this, I'd like to discuss a potential relationship - but let's cross that bridge when we get there."

While you want your Sugar Daddy to know that you require a foundation, you don't want to make him feel pressured or defensive. That's why this script works so well. Let him know that it's on your mind, and that you will come to that eventually. If played appropriately, your Sugar Daddy will bring it up on his own and make you an offer – which means you won't even need to ask!

Open up the communication with your Sugar Daddy.

After all, it's not about you. What does your Sugar Daddy want? Does he want to give you advice? Does he want to spend more time with a like-minded person? Find out what your Sugar Daddy wants, and use that when creating a relationship.

Number Two Lame Excuse: You Can't Justify What You Want

If you find yourself mulling these thoughts over and over: "I haven't been dating him very long," "I am already getting an allowance" – then you might not be able to justify what you want.

Careful, we have a tendency to undervalue ourselves.

You're not easily replaceable – you're a unique woman with a lot to offer a Sugar Daddy. And if you don't believe that, look at it from a practical standpoint.

Your Sugar Daddy doesn't want to spend a lot of time and money replacing you.

It's panic-inducing to him to think that he'll have to go through all the effort to find another Sugar Baby like you.

You have more leverage than you think - and you can actually increase it (more on that later).

Second, if you're not a top Sugar Baby, there's only one solution...Become one!

You can do this, and it doesn't take long I'm not saying anyone can be a Sugar Baby, but a Sugar Baby who is in a relationship can increase their wealth. It's your responsibility to make this happen, not your Sugar Daddy (use the earlier scripts I mentioned.)

Number Three Lame Excuse: Negotiating an Increase Isn't Possible in My Situation

Many Sugar Babies think that since they already in a relationship, they can't possibly negotiate asking for more than what they are currently receiving. You may believe that it's a valid reason why you can't ask. But how do you know it's true? Have you tested it?

It's okay to want more from your Sugar Daddy...and honestly, he's going to expect it from you. That's why it's important for you to learn how to negotiate an increase in a way that improves and strengthens your Sugar Daddy relationship. You'll learn about this in just a moment!

If you want to change where you are right now...

And you want to start enjoying the Sugar Baby lifestyle you deserve then move forward to my next step!

Get What You Want by Exploiting Every Sugar Daddy's Greatest Weakness

There's something that you really want from your Sugar Daddy – and for some reason, he's just not giving in.

Whether you need that next semester's tuition bill paid or you're just dying to sport the latest necklace from Tiffany's, any great Sugar Daddy should be willing to please his Sugar Baby. But sometimes a Sugar Daddy just needs a push in the right direction. And if you know just what direction to push him in, then you can get what you want…

…Every time!

What's the secret to this winning power over your Sugar Daddy? You just need to manipulate his great weakness: *his desire for pleasure!*

No matter how powerful or important your Sugar Daddy may be, he's still a man – and men love feeling like their pleasure is the number one thing on a woman's mind. That desire for pleasure doesn't have to have an intimate connotation either; in fact, something as simple as a compliment or a thoughtful gesture can go a long way towards pleasing your Sugar Daddy.

Here are a few ideas to get you going:

1. Love to cook? Invite your Sugar Daddy over for a sumptuous home-cooked feast, complete with a decadent dessert.

2. If there's a book that your Sugar Daddy has been dying to read, why not pick it up for him at the bookstore? Or if he has a favorite topic buy a book and read it and surprise him with your interest in his interests.

3. Compliment your Sugar Daddy! Let him know that you can tell he's been working out, or just compliment him on the way he wears a suit. A few kind words go a long way!

4. Devote 100% of your attention to him. Flatter him, laugh at his jokes, and tell him how much you appreciate his company, tell him you need his opinion or ideas – you'll get what you want from your Sugar Daddy in no time flat!

How Powerful Is Your Sugar Baby Smile?

The short answer is this: the most powerful weapon you own!

You know just how important it is to make a good first impression – and a smile is the most powerful weapon in your impression-making arsenal. Think about it this way: a smile can make you seem like the coolest and most confident woman in the room, no matter what situation you find yourself in. From scary job interviews to first dates, a smile can turn any potentially awkward or nerve-wracking scenario into a fun and friendly affair.

Well, this same rule applies to your Sugar Baby smile!

It's easy to forget that behind every powerful and wealthy Sugar Daddy is a regular man who's nervous about making a good first impression on you. After all, you're a gorgeous, smart and funny woman – and that combination can reduce any man into a bundle of nerves.

Studies have shown that when we don't smile, our peers assume that we're unfriendly or uncomfortable with our surroundings. In the Sugar Daddy/Sugar Baby relationship, having a constant frown on your face can make your Sugar Daddy feel as though you'd rather be anywhere but there. Just the simple act of smiling can make all of the difference in making your Sugar Daddy feel warm, comfortable and accepted. Also add some warm occasional eye contact as you are flashing that million-dollar smile.

Additionally, Sugar Daddies are naturally attracted to Sugar Babies who appear happy, enthusiastic and content. Put yourself in your Sugar Daddy's shoes: would you rather be sitting across from a glum woman who appears miserable, or a bubbly and enthusiastic Sugar Baby who has an appetite for life?

The answer's pretty obvious, isn't it?

No matter if you're going on your first Sugar Daddy meeting or your twentieth, don't forget to show those pearly whites. You'll be amazed at the difference it can make to your Sugar Daddy's mood!

18 Negotiate Your Relationship

How to Talk to Your Sugar Daddy About Money

Talking about money in general is uncomfortable. But talking about money with your Sugar Daddy can be so awkward that many Sugar Babies would rather avoid the conversation altogether! But if you want to be a successful Sugar Baby, you absolutely need to have that conversation with your Sugar Daddy. Because if you can't talk about it with your Sugar Daddy, then it's almost a guarantee that you won't get everything from you want from your relationship.

Remember that awkward feeling of asking for what you want? Sure, you and potential Sugar Daddy might have had an occasional chat about the relationship. But when you're getting serious—whether you're just starting out or dating or just at a point where you are not getting what you want and it is affecting how you feel about the relationship—it's important to spend some time talking about your relationship and your goals.

Talking about money with your Sugar Daddy might sound painful, but I promise you it doesn't have to be awkward. It can actually bring you closer together—if you know what to ask and how to go about it.

Specific tactics aren't as important as your attitude going in. The key is to start by asking for his advice. Yes, even if you don't need it! The goal should be to agree that you are focusing on each other's needs and not just what you are seeking to gain from the relationship. You need to emphasize that you are genuinely interested in him as a person and not as an ATM. That's it!

It is all about figuring out ways to mutual benefit from each other in the relationship.

When you sit down, start by talking about your goals. What do you want? What kind of lifestyle do you expect? This will be a sensitive conversation because nobody wants to be judged. But remember, keep an open mind. Ask him, "How do you envision the relationship? What are you looking for out of it?" Get him to show you his hand first. And then it's your turn.

The most important goal of this conversation is to set up the foundation in which it would be both mutually beneficial for both.

How to Negotiate With Your Sugar Daddy

Asking for what you want shouldn't feel like a mystery, or an anxiety-inducing attack. The biggest mistake Sugar Babies make is not to negotiate at all. They are happy to find a relationship and take whatever offer is put on the table by the potential Sugar Daddy and leave thousands on the table.

When we ask for what we want, we're afraid of being portrayed as a gold digger or an escort…so we don't say anything and let the Sugar Daddies guide the relationship.

Whatever you do, don't fall into this trap!

But before you can start getting that extra money, you need to answer this pivotal question: what does an allowance mean to you? Negotiation is one of the most powerful ways to earn what you deserve. To put it bluntly, Sugar Babies suck at negotiation and leave tons of opportunities on the table each year.

So how can you improve your negotiation skills – and start getting what you want out of the relationship?

Negotiation is about overcoming your fears, understanding your value, and communicating it persuasively to others. If you can master a simple allowance negotiation, you can master so many other areas of life. Now, there will be some Sugar Babies who will want simple tactics. "Taylor," they'll say, "Gimme some tactics! What are the magic words to use to penetrate their minds? If you just tell me the right words, I'll be unstoppable!"

I want to teach you the deeper strategy behind negotiating getting you what you want. Anyone can memorize a list of words. But the pattern among the most successful Sugar Babies is the ability to deeply understand what's going on behind the scenes within their Sugar Daddies' minds.

How do you change your approach if your Sugar Daddy balks at what you want? What if he flat-out says, "No, not going to do that?" Here are the techniques you should use when negotiating:

Don't feel guilty about asking for what you want! Sugar Babies shouldn't apologize or worry about how the potential Sugar Daddy will feel when wanting to discuss what you want out of the relationship. Feeling guilty lessens the weight of you getting what you want. Stay away from saying things like, "I'm sorry to ask for this, but I feel..." Your Sugar Daddy is well aware this is part of the whole deal. In fact you will gain a measure of respect if you negotiate in a way that is assertive but not confrontational. This will preserves his dignity while still getting you what you deserve.

Don't feel guilty *period*. You are already being valued less because you are a Sugar Baby. Be confident.

And what if he says "no"? Say, 'I'm surprised that you would offer anything less than what I am asking." Don't get mad at him, just be measured and direct the conversation to a resolution.

Don't use the words, "I feel..." It may be second nature to express how you feel about a topic, but those words need to be kept out of negotiations. Most negotiations are about facts, data and information. Once you talk about feelings, you lose credibility.

If your potential Sugar Daddy says "no" to what you want, respond with questions. Say: "What about {insert what you are seeking} is not palatable to you?"

Allow enough room to permit them to make at least three concessions to get what you want.

If, during the process, the potential Sugar Daddy presents something surprising (or outright shocking), maintain composure. Then walk away from the table and come back. Always let the potential Sugar Daddy assume that you know your value and that you're not desperate or willing to take whatever that is offered to you.

Because you're *not* desperate!

The point of a negotiation is to drive the conversation to an agreement. Saying "no" closes off the conversation and makes it difficult to start back up.

Let's give an example to help highlight this point.

You are seeking the help of your Sugar Daddy financial generosity to help fund your business and need $2K but your potential Sugar Daddy tells you he can only assist with $1K.

Instead of saying no. Ask him "What is it about this figure that's difficult for you?

Or, try something like this: "Having talked about helping me with my business the amount needed will help me {Insert how it will help you}. What is it about this figure that's difficult for you?"

Sometimes it might not be in their budget. And sites that outlines a Sugar Daddy contribution doesn't reflect realistic amounts.

However, if you open the conversation it will allow you to see what it is that they can do and possibly could be beneficial to you and your lifestyle.

> "Always remember that you should value his advice not his money. His money might be limited, but once you know what he knows, your opportunities are unlimited." – Alicia Dunums

Continue the conversation with phrases such as "I hear what you are saying," and "Tell me something about that." It's all about active listening and trust-building.

190

Now let's move forward to the last step...effective negotiation tips that will get your Sugar Daddy to give what you want!

Do You Know Your Sugar Baby Value?

When it comes to your Sugar Baby/Sugar Daddy relationship, there's only one truth that you need to know: if you don't set your value, your Sugar Daddy will.

And whether he does it on purpose or not, he's going to set that value pretty darn low.

Unfortunately, many novice Sugar Babies make the mistake of letting their Sugar Daddies take the reins in determining their overall value. Perhaps they inherently believe that they're not worth much, or maybe they're too afraid to speak up for fear of turning off their Sugar Daddies.

Whatever the case may be, deciding your own Sugar Baby value will determine whether you go on shopping sprees at Nordstrom, or are reduced to buying last season's shoes at Payless. Prevent this disaster from happening by using these tips and techniques:

- **Determine Your Market Value.** It might feel strange quantifying your qualities and characteristics, but you certainly don't want your Sugar Daddy to do it for you! To determine your market value, consider the qualities that make you unique and fabulous. Do you have a way with words? Can you dance with the best of them? Let your Sugar Daddy know that you have plenty of characteristics that make you unique – and he'll have to pay for the privilege of experiencing them.

- **Establish Your Personal Value.** You're a smart, funny and eclectic woman – so don't downgrade your own personal value! Write down the positive personality traits that make you so special. It will remind yourself that you're worth every penny that your Sugar Daddy spends on you.

- **Communicate Your Expectations.** Of course, none of this introspection really matters unless you communicate your expectations to your Sugar Daddy. Provide him with a specific budget, and you'll be taking the upper hand in establishing your own worth.

How to Get What You're Worth

When I ran a survey, I asked Sugar Babies, "Do you feel like you're getting less than what you want out of your Sugar Daddy Relationship?"

100% of Sugar Babies said "YES!"

I then asked those same people to explain why, and they said:

"Sugar Daddies won't pay what I'm seeking, so I lower what I am asking."

"Sugar Babies are asking for less than I do, so I lowered what I want to match."

"I don't believe I could ask more for what I want."

Sound familiar?

It turns out that most Sugar Babies who struggle with getting what they want have these same problems.

I can't persuade Sugar Daddies to give me what I want. The Sugar Daddies that I'm attracting can't afford me.

What is really going on here? Why do Sugar Babies feel like this? Do you feel like this?

If you are feeling like this you likely make one or all of these 3 mistakes

#1 You are Attracting the wrong Sugar Daddies

There is such a thing as targeting the wrong Sugar Daddies

#2 You are not demonstrating your Sugar Baby Value

If you are asking for something specific such as an allowance than it is up to you to describe to your Sugar Daddy your worth. Your worth is perceived through his perception. Your perception is contrived by how you portray yourself. If you only mentioned what you are seeking and you make no mention of how you can provide them of what they are looking for. You are handling yourself as a commodity and being treated as such.

#3 You are comparing yourself to other Sugar Babies

Do you think successful Sugar Babies worry about what others are getting? They are focused on what they want out of this lifestyle. They observe how their Sugar Baby competition is coming across.

I'm betting you are likely feeling you are the best Sugar Baby a Sugar Daddy can have.

Which of these 3 mistakes have you made and what things are you worried about?

So, what can you do?

The first thing you can do is get ultra specific on your value that you offer/provide.

Stop talking about what you want and focus on your Sugar Daddy needs and establish your perception. Position yourself as the Sugar Baby for him and in turn he will provide you what you want but above all make sure you are attracting the right Sugar Daddies that can provide you what you want and are seeking the same thing from the relationship.

Warning: HIV and Condoms

"Fifteen percent of new HIV cases have been found in adults over fifty. Other STDs higher too. Older men don't like condoms – but no one likes AIDS or STDs." – Dr. Ruth

"Condoms are less likely to be used in Sugar Daddy relationships than in other non-marital sexual partnerships...Condoms are also less likely to be used in relationships with large age differences (ten or more years) and in relationships that involve large amounts of material assistance." – Leila Darabi

Don't let your Sugar Daddy negotiate with you about not using condoms. Receiving money (allowance) and/or presents can lead to poor judgment calls and life-altering consequences.

Sugar Daddies will try to trick you into having unprotected sex. "Condoms are uncomfortable." "I can't feel anything with a condom." "I want to be closer to you."

"If you want this relationship with me, you'll do it." "I promise I'll pull out in time."

"If the condom is actually causing the guy discomfort, it means two things: he has the wrong size and/or he's sensitive to the latex, spermicide, or other chemicals used. Fear not, there is a condom for him out there. There are many, many brands of condoms to choose from, often with silly names and/or fruit flavors. At this point, you could stock an entire Wal-Mart entirely with condom brands. (I believe there's a brand that glows in the dark at this point.) There are many types for guys of all sizes, even those with sensitive wangs. Ask him specifically what is making him uncomfortable. If he's legitimately uncomfortable, there are many solutions. Why not go to the store with him and pick out a brand together?"

Yes, condoms aren't 100% effective in preventing unwanted pregnancies and STDs, but they are 100% more effective than the pull-out method. "The condom is uncomfortable" is never a good excuse. You know what is more uncomfortable? The feeling of a burning sensation when you pee.

19 Your New Life

E very woman dreams of having a powerful and wealthy man at her beck and call – and if you're a successful Sugar Baby, then this dream can quickly become reality! However, there's a difference between *attracting* a Sugar Daddy and *keeping* a Sugar Daddy who's so wealthy and powerful that the city's at his fingertips. And once you've attracted this caliber of Sugar Daddy, you need to know how to wrap him around your finger, allowing you to live the luxurious lifestyle you've always dreamed of.

So how can you make this happen?

Remember the number one rule: a high-quality Sugar Daddy is looking for a woman with whom he can have *an emotional and intellectual connection.*

How to Stimulate Your Sugar Daddy's Mind

As a beautiful woman, it's easy to capture your Sugar Daddy's eye. But do you know how to capture your Sugar Daddy's mind?

That's right: if you want to turn a casual Sugar Daddy fling into a full-blown relationship (with all of the amazing benefits!), then you need to learn every trick of the trade to capturing his mind. Why is so important to place an emphasis on his mind, rather than, say, his eye? The reason is simple: as a wealthy and powerful man, your Sugar Daddy is constantly bombarded with tons of beautiful women who dress in the latest fashions. And while this may be temporarily pleasing, it's the woman who captured his mind that will take first place in his life.

So how can you capture your Sugar Daddy's mind? Simple: use these tips and techniques!

- Don't emphasize your body. Sure, you can show it off – but if that's all you can offer your Sugar Daddy, then he'll become disinterested pretty quickly.

- Talk about your goals and interests. If you plan on opening your own veterinary practice one day, tell your Sugar Daddy about it. Wealthy and powerful men are extremely attracted to women who have their own thing going on, so if you're an ambitious lady, flaunt it!

- Be a little mysterious. Sugar Daddies are constantly fighting off women who are throwing themselves at them – but you can bet that if you tease a little and hold back, he'll be dying to know more about you.

Once you capture your Sugar Daddy's mind, you'll be introduced to the kind of luxurious lifestyle you deserve!

How to Stroke Your Sugar Daddy's Ego

Your Sugar Daddy could be the most important and powerful man in the city, but that doesn't change the fact that he's still a red-blooded man. And if there's one thing that women need to learn about men, it's this: there are two things that all men love a woman to stroke. You can easily guess one of them. The other is just as important: Rich and powerful love it when you stroke their *egos*.

Your Sugar Daddy has worked long and hard to get to the top of his game, and now he wants to sit back and bask in all he's done. But that doesn't mean you should fall over yourself to give him false compliments – after all, most people can see right through that type of flattery. If you want to stroke your Sugar Daddy's ego, follow these simple tips to give him the ego boost that results in more gifts for you!

- Men are very competitive creatures – and no one is more competitive than a successful Sugar Daddy. The next time you're out on a date with him, go up to the bar and mildly flirt with the bartender while you order drinks. Then come back to your Sugar Daddy. He'll be so proud that such a gorgeous and intelligent woman only has eyes for him!

- Ask him for his advice. Men love dishing out advice, so your Sugar Daddy will jump at the chance to help you through a tough problem. Let him know just how much you appreciate his great advice for an extra ego boost.

- Get your hands involved in your conversation! By continually touching his arm and placing your hand on his, you're essentially saying that you find him incredibly irresistible – and that's a surefire ego booster for any man!

How to Create an Unbreakable Bond With Your Sugar Daddy

Finding the Sugar Daddy of your dreams is only half of the battle – because once you find him, you have to hold onto him!

Powerful and wealthy men will always be in demand. From their busy careers to their frantic social lives, it can be tough to create a strong bond with your Sugar Daddy due to so much external pressure. But you know that once you've forged that bond, you and your Sugar Daddy can stand against the world together.

So how can you create that unbreakable bond in the first place? Simple: by following these easy-to-use tips and techniques!

- Focus on what you have in common with your Sugar Daddy. Do you both share a passion for politics? Do you both enjoying going to the theater together? By highlighting what you have in common, he'll be reminded of you whenever he does his favorite activity.

- Try to see your Sugar Daddy beyond his job and finances. Sure, a major perk to having a Sugar Daddy is the fact that you get plenty of gifts; but if you want to forge an unbreakable bond, you need to connect with him as a person – not as an ATM!

- If you have a problem and need some advice, turn to your Sugar Daddy for help. Sugar Daddies love feeling like their opinions are valued – and if you turn to him for advice, he'll start to feel like your mentor in addition to your benefactor. But never dump your problems in his lap. Never demand that he solve a problem for you. Remember that one of the key things that he values about your relationship is that you provide an environment *free of stress*. If he wanted stress he'd go to the office or go back home! As his Sugar Baby, it's your job to ensure that every time he sees you, it's like going on a romantic vacation.

Your Sugar Daddy can be one of the most important relationships you'll ever have in your life – so make sure it's an unbreakable one!

Getting Your Sugar Daddy to Put You First

As a Sugar Baby, you know your Sugar Daddy is a busy man. Between his career, his family and his friends, it's a wonder that he can even find space in his day to spend with his favorite Sugar Baby!

But although you understand his scheduling needs, you'd still like to see your Sugar Daddy more often. After all, he's a smart, funny and interesting man – not to mention he treats you to the most fabulous nights out!

So how can you let your Sugar Daddy know that you'd like to come first without seeming needy or demanding? Simple – just use these tips to let your Sugar Daddy know that you're ready to be put first:

- You obviously like spending time with your Sugar Daddy, so why not tell him how much fun you're having? Your Sugar Daddy might simply be holding back because he doesn't know how you feel. Insert a comment such as "I really enjoy spending time with you," and watch how quickly he makes time for you.

- Keep the lines of communication open. If your Sugar Daddy keeps canceling plans on you, let him know (in the nicest way possible!) just how excited you were to spend time with him. He might not even realize he's not spending enough time with you; therefore, a gentle reminder is all he needs to set things right.

- If your Sugar Daddy still won't put you first, be a little less available. By always being available for your Sugar Daddy, you're sending him a message that you'll always drop plans for him.

Give him a taste of his own medicine – he'll come around!

A Red Flag That Tells Your Sugar Daddy That You Are Not the One

When it comes to controlling the relationship, there's no doubt that Sugar Babies have plenty of say. From deciding when to become intimate to setting up a budget for the relationship, the Sugar Baby tends to run the show.

However, there's one pivotal hurdle that every Sugar Baby needs to jump over before they can win the hearts of their Sugar Daddies – and that's convincing him that *you're the one.*

For Sugar Daddies, picking their ideal Sugar Baby is a long process. After all, they're looking for more of an emotional investment than a sexual one – so they need to be sure that their Sugar Baby is worth the effort.

And if you want to convince your Sugar Daddy that you're the one, then you need to avoid this major red flag:

Asking for too much, too soon.

The Sugar Daddy/Baby relationship is ultimately a financial one. But that doesn't mean you should immediately demand endless amounts of gifts and presents just after one date. Instead, a Sugar Daddy is looking for a Sugar Baby who is just as invested in finding an emotional connection as he is. Expecting gifts and payments too soon cuts off that emotional connection that's so important to the Sugar Daddy, not to mention it's a major red flag that you'll disappear as soon as you find a wealthier Sugar Daddy! If you want to keep your new Sugar Daddy around, take it easy with the gift requests at first. Only after you've determined that you're a good match should you mention any bills you want paid – and he'll be far more likely to pay them for you!

Three Key Tips That Will Open The Doors To More Sugar Daddies

You may be getting a few messages from potential Sugar Daddies – but what can you do to get more responses?

Sugar Babies who get a flood of emails from Sugar Daddies have their pick from these generous and wealthy men. And that's exactly the position you want to be in. But short of advertising yourself in neon lights on Sugar Daddy dating websites, what can you do to attract more Sugar Daddies?

It's simple: Use the three key tips that I've outlined. How great would it feel if you made one simple tweak to your Sugar Daddy Dating, and saw an immediate increase in the number of potential Sugar Daddies? I know, silly question. It would feel great. Now what if there were three simple tweaks... each of which could have that same effect?

You'd stop reading this book right now and use each of 'em. Right? Right! What Sugar Baby wouldn't want to be more successful with Sugar Daddies? The question is... what are those three simple tweaks?

I call them the "**Sugar Baby Psych Master Keys.**"

Smart Sugar Babies who want to increase their success rate with Sugar Daddies must master the fields of human behavior and psychology. Understanding that simple insight has worked for me and for countless other *Sugar Daddy Formula* members.

The Sugar Daddies you're talking to are still men — and they have very specific needs. And that's why the following three Keys are so powerful. Each tweak is based off of proven psychological principles that have been proven today and will likely remain true for the foreseeable future.

So, without further ado, let's jump right in.

Key #1: Sugar Daddies Actually Like Helping You

Newsflash: Sugar Daddies don't help you because you label yourself a Sugar Baby. Sugar Daddies provide for you because of how you make them feel. And it gets better...

When Sugar Daddies offer to help they do it because they *want* to. When they offer to help it takes on a different meaning: it gives them a sense of helping you when you're in need, and they're the only person who can help. It's kind of like playing the hero...and you're the damsel in distress!

Key #2: The Secret to Growing Your Sugar Daddy Relationship is Earning Your Sugar Daddy's Trust

Your objective is to build the trust within the relationship. If there is no trust in the relationship Sugar Daddies will not do anything for you.

Period.

So what can you do to build trust in your Sugar Daddy relationship? Simple: talk about your feelings. Share secrets with him. Let him know that he's the only one who knows this about you. The more you open up to him, the more the trust will grow – and that's key in creating Sugar Daddy intimacy.

Key #3: How Mystery Helps You Score More Sugar Daddies

If you reveal all that there is to know about you in your profile ad, why should a Sugar Daddy get to know you? Let him get to know you and reveal a bit over time about you. Be a never-ending book to your Sugar Daddy. Keep a mystery about you.

For example, do you speak another language? If so, go to a restaurant where you can speak it and be alluring in that way. Do you play a particular sport that your Daddy plays? Then set up a game for the two of you and surprise him with your skills.

Your Allure creates mystery, which in turn sparks desire. That leads to a curious Sugar Daddy, which inevitable leads to a sustained relationship. So go ahead and withhold some information, because your Sugar Daddy relationship will definitely benefit from it!

Some Common Problems My Clients Have In Sugar Baby Relationships

1. Keeping the relationship fresh

If you've been in a long-term relationship, you know the story: after your honeymoon phase, things get a little less exciting and a little more predictable. Sometimes you work through it, sometimes you don't.

So if you've snagged the perfect Sugar Daddy, how do you keep the relationship fresh over time?

I could write a whole book about this, and you've already learned a lot of great tips in this book that can help you out with this. Here's one that I haven't talked about yet:

Always come up with creative positive surprise.

If you've followed the advice from the "Know Your Sugar Daddy" chapter, this should be really easy. For example, I had a Sugar Daddy that used to be in the music industry on the production side, and every time he talked about music, I could hear it in his voice the love affair he has with it. So while we were traveling out of town I purchased tickets to a live music venue for him. And guess what? He was in heaven! He even knew the musician in the band, which added to the experience. I was right by his side and bonded even more with him.

2. Dealing with jealousy

Another problem my clients have is dealing with the intense jealousy they feel, and the jealousy their Sugar Daddies have about them.

Here's the key: always establish the ground rules early so there are not any shattered expectations. Communication is the most important thing to establish with your Sugar Daddy. Not communicating basically guarantees that jealousy will come up.

Also, the type of Sugar Daddy you are with will make jealousy more or less likely. The status of your Sugar Daddy also makes a difference – a married Sugar Daddy is going to be a lot less jealous than a single Sugar Daddy.

If you want some more advice on dealing with your Sugar Daddy's jealousy, go back and read the section about how to handle having a boyfriend in addition to your Sugar Daddy.

3. Getting comfortable in new social situations

If you're with a Sugar Daddy, you may spend time in so-cial scenes that you haven't before. This is intimidating for a lot of Sugar Babies, and my clients come to me all the time asking about what they should do to prepare themselves for new social situations.

Here's the key: preparation. The more you prepare, the easier things will be when you actually show up. Do your research. The internet is an incredible tool. Basi-cally you have all the information you could ever want on any social scene at the tip of your fingers.

When you actually show up, observe others. See if you can find the people who seem to know what they are doing, and mimic what they do. Plus you shouldn't be afraid of asking others for advice.

4. Your own age and appearance

It's true, you're going to get older. My clients freak out about getting older and becoming less "attractive" and think that they won't be able to get a high quality Sugar Daddy or keep him around.

Here's the thing: it doesn't matter. There are Sugar Ba-bies all over the place who are older than you and aren't as pretty as you. Nevertheless, they are able to get and keep amazing Sugar Daddies because they embody the traits that you've been reading about in this book.

Offer more to your Sugar Daddy than your body. Dress appropriately and behave as such. And of course, take care of yourself as much as you can.

5. Dealing with haters

Let's be real: there are a lot of Sugar Baby haters. You may be called an escort. You may be called a trophy. Heck, they may even call you a slut. But you know what… it doesn't matter.

All you need to do is be true to yourself and expect love from those around you. If you aren't getting the love that you deserve, then maybe you need to shut some people out. There are no shortage of amazing people out there to surround yourself with.

That said, discretion is your friend. There is no need to go around bragging about your Sugar Daddy relationship. Believe in what you're doing, do your thing, and let haters be hating!

How to Test Your Sugar Daddy without Turning Him Away from You

For many Sugar Babies, it can be difficult to determine just what their Sugar Daddies are prepared to do for them. So if you're curious to see how far your Sugar Daddy will really go for you, then why not set up a little test for him?

To test your Sugar Daddy without losing him, use smaller requests rather than grander gestures if you want to determine just how far he'll go for you. That way, he won't realize that you're testing him – and you won't have to deal with a Sugar Daddy that's so angry that he wants to leave you! Try asking if he can cover an unexpected bill for you.

Remember this: If you think that taking off your clothes will guarantee that he'll say yes, then think again. Easy availability limits your Sugar Daddy's desire to do more for you. Additionally, it can undercut your Sugar Daddy's respect for you. A Sugar Baby should never equate sex with getting more things – after all, that's heading into escort territory!

Instead, appeal to his emotional and intellectual side. Ask calmly and politely; if he says no, don't pout. It might be time to find another Sugar Daddy to supplement your extra expenses – or a new Sugar Daddy that's willing to do more for you!

Keeping Your Sugar Daddy in Suspense

Unfortunately, many Sugar Babies go about the mystery in suspense in all the wrong way. They keep up the allure for a few weeks or a few months, until the Sugar Daddy starts getting comfortable with them. Once they've reached that level of intimacy, however, Sugar Babies throw all mystery out of the window.

And Sugar Daddies are suddenly looking around for a new Sugar Baby that will keep them in suspense. Don't let this happen to you. Keep your Sugar Daddy always looking for more with these two important tips:

1. If your Sugar Daddy reveals an interest that you share, speak up – but don't lay everything down on the table. For example, if your Sugar Daddy loves golf, and you're good at the game, don't tell him over dinner. Instead, take him to the golf course, and let your skills speak for themselves.

2. Treat yourself like a book with several chapters. Instead of letting your Sugar Daddy cruise through all of the chapters in one sitting, carefully reveal your interests, passions and skills over time. Use this method, and he'll constantly be excited for what you'll reveal to him.

As you can see, keeping your Sugar Daddy in suspense requires being a little mysterious – but I guarantee that he'll be absolutely gaga for you if you do it!

20 Understanding Your Sugar Daddy Personality

There's no denying that there are certain men you're drawn to. Well, when it comes to Sugar Daddies, the exact same rule applies. If you want to find your ultimate Sugar Baby success, then you need to know precisely which type of Sugar Daddy you hope to meet. Think of it like the traditional dating world: you have your certain standards, and anyone who falls below those standards will be jettisoned out of your dating pool.

Many Sugar Babies are hesitant to clearly define what they'd like from their Sugar Daddies, and which ones they're more compatible with. And I'll admit, being showered with gifts and financial benefits can make it easy for a Sugar Baby to write off incompatibility.

But think of it this way: your Sugar Daddy could be the richest man in the world — but if the two of you have a fundamental flaw in your relationship, it's never going to work out.

For me, I detest a controlling man. In my Sugar Daddy dating past, I've been with men who had tons of cash — and weren't afraid to spend it on me — but in return, they expected me to be at their beck and call 24/7. Because I didn't understand my Sugar Baby goals and Sugar Daddy personalities, I put up with it for a lot longer than I should have before I broke free.

If there are certain aspects to a man that you just can't put up with, don't throw your standards away just because your Sugar Daddy has tons of cash. It will make you feel guilty — and besides, these types of relationships never work out. Even if I had stayed with my controlling Sugar Daddies, we would have ended the relationships at some point because we just had different expectations.

So fellow Sugar Babies, learn from me: know exactly what Sugar Daddy personalities you're compatible with so you can find your ideal Sugar Daddy faster.

21 Attracting Legitimate Sugar Daddies

A hhh, I know this is certainly a subject that many Sugar Babies want to talk about. And whether you're new to the Sugar Baby dating game or an experienced Sugar Baby, I bet you've had an encounter with what seemed to be a legitimate Sugar Daddy, only to quickly discover that he was an average guy playing you. Or you ended up with a Sugar Daddy who absolutely refused to address your needs within the relationship, like my previous Sugar Daddy who didn't want to help me pay for formal attire for *his party*.

It's unfortunate, but it can happen. But here's where I come in – this won't happen to you if you know the proper steps to finding a legitimate Sugar Daddy. And believe it or not, it doesn't begin with the contents of his bank account.

First, you'll need to understand your own concepts of what money is. How much is a lot to you? A few hundred dollars? A few thousand? To many wealthy Sugar Daddies, that could either be pocket change or a big chunk of change – it all depends on their personality type.

Once you've decided on a ballpark figure of what you would like from your Sugar Daddy, you can go about asking for it directly, or figuring it out for yourself.

What do I mean here? Well, here's where you can play detective.

If you want to get a better idea of what you can expect from your Sugar Daddy, do a little online research about his company. If you know his official role, research average salaries in similar companies (monster.com is a great resource for that).

Finally, take a look at his lifestyle. Does he travel a lot? Does he own a lot of real estate? Is he always going to the best bars and clubs?

You can find out this information by asking him questions. Not only will this provide you with the info you need, but your attentions will also make him feel flattered.

The bottom line is this: by asking the right questions, you can find out about a Sugar Daddy's financial standings, which will help you determine a proper and realistic allowance if that is what you are seeking or if he is able to provide you with what you want.

Never Give a Sugar Daddy More Than He Gives You

Have you ever found yourself falling for a Sugar Daddy you wanted get to know better – only to find yourself sleeping with him before an relationship has been made? It's an unfortunate but common occurrence within the world of Sugar Daddy dating. If you want to become a successful Sugar Baby, you must avoid falling into this trap. Focusing on what a Sugar Daddy wants and ingratiating yourself in this way may feel like the natural thing to do, but it's the worst way to try to make a Sugar Daddy fall for you.

Being "nice" and "understanding" and "a good sport" won't get you where you want to go. If you want to get to where you need to be, embrace this tip: don't give a Sugar Daddy more than he gives you.

Most of us only know how to give. We give for lots of reasons – because we're taught that's the way to get to attract a man (it isn't), and because deep down, it feels uncomfortable asking for what you want and you allow your potential Sugar Daddy to put the value on the relationship.

But Sugar Daddies can't read your mind.

Reread that: Sugar Daddies can't read your mind.

Just because they are on a Sugar Daddy site doesn't mean they automatically know what it is that you want.

You want to inspire his emotional desire for you. Allow your potential Sugar Daddy to prove himself to *you*. Don't feel compelled to have sex with a Sugar Daddy in hopes of receiving things, only to end up waiting by the phone or checking your email to see if he reached out to you. To advance your Sugar Daddy relationship, he needs to woo you. And believe me: you're worth wooing.

22 Why Settle for just One Sugar Daddy?

C an a successful Sugar Baby have more than one Sugar Daddy? This question depends on what you're looking to gain out of this lifestyle. What does success look like to you?

Let's look at it in a different perspective: What are your goals? What are you hoping to achieve out of this lifestyle? Does your current Sugar Daddy provide you what you are looking for?

When I started Sugar Daddy dating I didn't know what I wanted out of this lifestyle but I wanted to be better of than where I was. In the midst of it all I became strategic about it. All men are Sugar Daddies. It's a matter of finding the right one to provide you what you want.

Not all Sugar Daddies are created equal. Why would I settle for a Sugar Daddy who can just provide me what I wanted with his financial generosity when I can have a Sugar Daddy to help accelerate my goals too? I have always been into business and the best fit for me would be a Business Sugar Daddy. I would use what he knows and also his contacts.

Make sense? Now, I can diversify my portfolio with other Sugar Daddies based on my goals.

23 The Top 10 Mistakes Sugar Babies Make

In reverse order, here are the top ten biggest mistakes made by aspiring Sugar Babies.

Mistake #10 - Thinking That Your Sugar Daddy Date Actually Meant Something

Have you ever had a potential Sugar Daddy say how much he likes you, how sexy you are, and how he's serious about finding a Sugar Baby like you? Ever have an amazing date where the chemistry was great, the conversation flowed, and you hooked up with him afterwards?

Have you ever had a man do all of these things and then not call? No, you're not crazy or delusional. The mistake is that you think that what a potential Sugar Daddy says on a date actually <u>means</u> something. It doesn't. It means he's being in the moment.

Before you get upset at me: I'm not faulting you for something terrible that he did. I'm saying that if 50% of great dates don't result in second dates, don't be too surprised when this happens to you.

The solution is not giving up on Sugar Daddy dating. It's about not getting too excited or emotionally involved with the hopes of entering in a relationship before it even starts and after a fun night. The only way you can tell how a potential Sugar Daddy really feels about you is by how quickly he follows up for another date.

Mistake #9 - Ignoring Your Own Intuition

How many times have you been across a table from some potential Sugar Daddy and found yourself wishing that you'd rather be anywhere else on earth? How many times have you felt deceived, angered, manipulated, or just plain turned off by the potential Sugar Daddy in front of you?

Now, how many times have you considered that it was actually <u>your fault</u> that he was sitting there?

I'm not blaming you. I've been there myself. But the common denominator in all your bad dates is not the awful Sugar Daddies themselves, but *you*. If you find yourself losing hope that there are any great Sugar Daddies out there, do yourself a favor and only go out with Sugar Daddies who truly interest you. Instead of meeting potentials in hopes of receiving what they may offer. This strategy will prevent most bad dates before they happen.

I know it sounds like I'm being harsh on you, but since you can't change how Sugar Daddies act, the only thing you can do is to make different decisions. If you screen Sugar Daddies better, you go out with fewer fakes. If you go out with fewer fakes, you won't feel nearly as bad about the Sugar Daddy dating process. And if you don't feel bad about the dating process, you're going to be a much happier Sugar Baby for that next amazing Sugar Daddy you meet!

Mistake #8 - Waiting for Sugar Daddies to Write You First

Have you ever sat in front of your computer, reading emails from undesirable Sugar Daddies, and asked yourself why the genuine Sugar Daddies never write to you? You look at your favorites list and wish you could say hi to them, but you know better. It's tradition: men approach women. And you wouldn't want to come across as desperate. After all, what Sugar Daddy wants a woman who's so needy that she has to write to him first?

Actually, all men do. They love it.

If you have a good photo, an interesting profile and you write a confident email, most Sugar Daddies will take notice. The key is in learning how to write a confident email. An email that grabs a Sugar Daddy and screams "Guess what? This is your lucky day!"

Mistake #7 - Expecting Him to Tell The Truth in His Profile (His Finances)

You don't like to be lied to. Nobody does. And once you've gone out with a man who claimed to make over $100K but is really making $35K, it's hard to keep dating. But haven't you ever done the same thing? (Lied.) The typical Sugar Baby exaggerates her age, and if she is in school.

I'm not defending it. I'm just saying it happens. So don't get too surprised or upset when it does. Save yourself some hearthake and start out thinking it all needs to be vetted in some way before you take it as true.

Mistake #6 - Thinking You're Now in a Sugar Relationship with the Sugar Daddy You've Met Online

Have you ever gone on an amazing date and saw that he was online right afterwards? Have you ever emailed a Sugar Daddy who seemed interested, then suddenly disappeared? Have you ever gotten intimate with a Sugar Daddy who never called again?

You're not alone. All of these things are common. So instead of taking it as a personal rejection each time a Sugar Daddy comes and goes, take a step back. Think of all the potential Sugar Daddies who have written to you that you weren't interested in. Imagine all of them taking it personally. It's ridiculous.

It's easy to forget how many choices Sugar Daddies have. It's easy to forget how many other Sugar Babies they're contacting. And if you think that you're exclusive with every new potential Sugar Daddy that gets you excited, you're in for a lot of disappointment.

Mistake #5 - Meeting for a Date to Save Time Without Seeing if You're Compatible from the Start

Have you ever spent a month talking to a Sugar Daddy online and discovered on the date that he wasn't looking for the same type of relationship you were looking for? I have. I remember vowing not to waste that kind of time on a potential Sugar Daddy ever again. You probably did, too. You probably started meeting Sugar Daddies right away to make sure that you had that "in-person chemistry." And at some point, on your tenth (or twentieth) bad date, you probably asked yourself, "Why do I even bother?"

Finding a Sugar Daddy online is *not* about meeting as many Sugar Daddies as quickly as possible. Moving quickly does not mean there is no screening. The only way to enjoy Sugar Daddy dating is by going out with fewer Sugar Daddies. It's far better to go on one comfortable date than five blind dates during the week.

Mistake #4 - Expecting That You'll Attract a Sugar Daddy Because You Labeled Yourself a Sugar Baby

You're sweet. You're fun. You're attractive. You have no trouble meeting men in real life. You figure that, with all your good qualities, Sugar Daddy dating should be a piece of cake. Except that's not how it's worked out. The only Sugar Daddies contacting you are little to be desired. There have to be better Sugar Daddies out there. Then how come they aren't writing?

Simple. Any Sugar Daddy who you think is a great catch has hundreds of options. And when a guy has that many choices, he's often going to search for younger women. Not always, but often. Why? Because he <u>can</u>. Focus your attentions on the men who you want to attract and would be subjective to your charm and you'll have far greater Sugar Baby success.

Mistake #3 - Trying to Stop the "Wrong" Sugar Daddies From Writing to You

Have you ever had a profile that just seemed to attract all the wrong Sugar Daddies? You want a man who is successful, and honest, and all you get are guys who lie. So, to stop them from wasting your time, you decide to spell it out in your profile: "If can't afford to give $X allowance, not seeking a mutual beneficial arrangement then don't bother writing." And yet they *still* keep on contacting you! What can you possibly do to stop these annoying men who can't read?

Nothing. Ignore them. Pity them. But don't try to stop them. After all, if you have any standards, most of your emails are going to be from the "wrong" Sugar Daddies. That's okay. They're allowed to write to you. And you're allowed to delete their email. You're going to get all sorts of men who are interested in you. Your job isn't to scare away the bad Sugar Daddies; it's to attract the good ones. And profiles with negative warnings to the "wrong" men only make you sound bad and self-absorbed.

Mistake #2 - Signing Up for a One-Month Subscription

Have you ever felt hopeless after a Sugar Daddy date that didn't go the way you wanted? Have you ever felt that time was running out? Have you ever wondered if there was a Sugar Daddy for you?

And even though you know how difficult it is to find a Sugar Daddy, you signed up for a one-month subscription to a paid Sugar Daddy site. One month! You're supposed to find a Sugar Daddy before you get your next phone bill! Clearly, you've created an unrealistic time-table. So while you may not want to date online forever, you're shortchanging yourself if you act as if you have only thirty days to find a Sugar Daddy.

Remind yourself why you want this lifestyle – it's hard to meet Sugar Daddies in real life.

Even though it may be tough and it may be frustrating, you have to remember one important thing if you are serious about this lifestyle: quitting is <u>not</u> an option.

Mistake #1 - Searching for the "Right" Sugar Daddy Dating Site

If a girlfriend told you that her biggest problem in losing weight was that she couldn't find the right gym, you'd probably shake your head. You know that it's not the gym, but your friend's dedication to using the gym that makes all the difference. Yet you may think that you can cure your Sugar Daddy dating blues just by choosing the right Sugar Daddy website. News-flash: *any* website with lots of men can be the right website; your success is ultimately determined by how you <u>use</u> that site.

230

You can Google all day long to find which site has the best Sugar Daddies. But at the end of the day, it's not the site that will determine your fate. It's you. There IS a man online who is looking for you right this very moment. The question is how committed you are to doing things right, persevering when things get tough, keeping a positive attitude, and turning yourself into a success story.

For every valuable tip out there on how to Sugar Daddy date, there are probably two mistakes to avoid. Keep away from the ten listed and you'll boost your success rate considerably. I also offer you personal advice, which you can have delivered straight to your inbox, if you haven't already subscribed for free to my newsletter at www.thesugardaddyformula.com.

24 How to Handle Rejection

I had a friend who looked to be a promising Sugar Baby. She was bright, witty, intelligent, and classy – all the characteristics Sugar Daddies look for. She had a good head on her shoulders, and she was prepared to do the work to find her perfect Sugar Daddy.

She thought she found him, but after a few dates, when she tried to discuss his financial contribution with him, he shot her down. Thanks to this rejection, she immediately withdrew from the Sugar Baby world – and it took her a long time to work up the strength to dive back in again.

Why am I telling you this? For one simple reason: too many Sugar Babies let themselves get thrown off by Sugar Daddy rejection. They think that failure is a bad thing, and that they'll never be the best Sugar Babies they want to be.

However, this is exactly the wrong way to approach Sugar Baby failure. In fact, I want to point out that failure should be planned for and even eagerly anticipated. I know that if I haven't been rejected by a few Sugar Daddies in my past, then I haven't done enough to truly learn on my Sugar Baby journey.

The bottom line is that rejection is a normal part of the Sugar Baby Process. Expect it. Manage it. Own it.

The trick is to prepare for failure before you even get rejected. Think of it as applying to college: you wouldn't just apply to your dream college and hope for the best, would you? Of course not. You'd spread out your options.

And that's exactly what you need to do with Sugar Daddy dating. Don't pin all your hopes on one man right in the beginning. You hold the cards. You have the power. Date as few or as many Sugar Daddies as what makes you feel comfortable. That way, when you encounter rejection – which you will – you'll already have a horde of other Sugar Daddies waiting to make you feel like the queen you are.

Whining and bashing the Sugar Daddy who rejected you is a great way to get stuck in the cycle of failure. It's just another way of protecting your ego – and there's no way you can possibly learn what you need to learn to become your best Sugar Baby possible.

It's easy to get angry at rejection. It's easy to get sad about rejection. But it's also easy to come up with a Plan B for rejection – and that's exactly where my above advice comes into play.

So what would you rather do: let failure knock you down, or eagerly learn from the experiences to become the best Sugar Baby possible?

I think the answer to that question is clear.

25 Beware of the Blogosphere!

S ugar Babies beware: You don't think your Potential Sugar Daddy is talking about you? Well, think again. What you read below was what was posted by a Sugar Daddy on the message board from an online forum.

Money is pretty much THE issue in landing sugar babes. Many of us have categorized these girls as to their motivation and life circumstances IOHO of course. They have educated themselves as to the going rate for escorts in this area and I think that is their starting point in negotiating with us. It totally depends on desperation I believe. Nando type I 's, for example, are desperately poor, usually have kids and no support, and can't work (or don't want to), and therefore will discount their services. Nevertheless, the rate here seems to be from $ to $$$. Vegas and the Left coast. Probably talking a lot higher. If you start high you will never be able to go down, so I think $$-$$.5 is reasonable *for an extended date-even overnight. If they want to be paid by the hour then you might as well see escorts and not risk falling for a SB. And the room is covered. GPS (golden pussy syndrome) exists and is alive and well unfortunately. If the girl wants way above the area rate then run like hell. Pussy is pussy and in no way shape or form is a dalliance worth over $$$ unless she is a virgin fashion model and you are popping that cherry for the first time.*

Long term costs are high and depend on the number of babies you want on your string and how often you want to play. With SB's you have higher costs than escorts because 1) you pay her 2) you cover the room. 3) you wine and dine her. 4) perhaps you bring a gift, so her fee is only the beginning. A golden rule that we all must follow. And many of us don't and get burned. Is. Do not pay in advance and expect her to work off the advance. I should repeat that in several different languages. I keep thinking that my Junk is so special that the baby will be honest and true to me. Wrong!"

Check out the Sugar Daddy thread! http://bit.ly/ydvnVC

A Smart Sugar Baby is always informed!

26 Your Sugar Baby
Action Plan

N ow is the time to take the lessons and secrets you've learned in this book and turn them into *action*!

Let's begin by reviewing your challenges, goals and dilemmas that may be stopping and preventing you from attracting your ideal Sugar Daddies.

Most important is, who are you? As this information will really apply to you. Are you a mother, college student? Divorced? Are you a woman wanting to enhance her lifestyle?

What do you have in common?

✓ *I'm new to the Sugar Daddy dating game, and I don't know how to get started.*

✓ *I can't seem to find the right Sugar Daddy. What am I doing wrong?*

✓ *I seem to attract great Sugar Daddies, but I just can't keep them interested.*

✓ *How do I know if a Sugar Daddy is worth keeping around?*

✓ *I met a great Sugar Daddy, but how can I make the bond last forever?*

✓ *How can I ask for what I want and get it?*

If you are just starting out, that is fine. If you have less than perfect Sugar Baby marketing skills that's okay too; otherwise you wouldn't be reading this book.

Who's perfect?

Nobody is perfect, Right? And we all want to make our Sugar Baby marketing effective and it's about focusing and finding an approach that works for us to effectively attract the Sugar Daddy we want. It's about finding ways to improve where you are now, and that is what we will be focusing on.

Before we learn how to improve our Sugar Baby marketing...

We need to know where we are in our Sugar Baby marketing right now.

A lot of Sugar Babies aren't aware of that. We're going to do an assessment so that you can see what you need to know and what you don't know so you know what to do next. I am going to introduce the 7 Secrets of Sugar Baby Marketing. This is my Sugar Baby marketing that I have been using and have narrowed down to these seven secrets. If you understand these areas you will be more effective at attracting potential Sugar Daddies, and if you don't understand them you will not attract the kind of Sugar Daddies you want.

Introducing the 7 Secrets of Sugar Baby Marketing:

1. The Game of Sugar Baby Marketing

This is my principle model of Sugar Baby Marketing. And I see Sugar Daddy dating as a game with rules where you get to keep score. A game with certain rules and structures, and you play it to win. And it's not something random. Sugar Babies do this all the time without any process or steps and are all over the place or one thing just leading to another thing. The great news is that Sugar Daddy dating is game and that there are certain rules.

241

I am going to give you a short version of the Sugar Daddy game and start in a locker room. And in this locker room is where we prepare our Sugar Baby marketing, our Sugar Baby message, our story and our allure so that we can target our potential Sugar Daddy. We need to figure out who our ideal Sugar Daddy is so that we position ourselves to communicate effectively to him.

A good part of our Sugar Baby marketing is to doing the preparation work and we will talk about those pieces as we go. And we want to work our way to home base. Your whole purpose is to go from home to first base, and you do this by communicating from what you have done in the locker room. When you get on first base you have the interest of a potential Sugar Daddy. He gets your message and he wants to know more and he responds to your profile to learn more.

So just understanding where you are in the Sugar Daddy game is essential but we really don't know where we are in the game.

Once we get to first base our job is to get to second base. Second base is where a potential Sugar Daddy wants to get to know you. Also called the Sugar Daddy experience in which your potential Sugar Daddy wants to get to know you. We don't go directly from first to second. Most of our Sugar Marketing happens between first and second base. So between first and second base is providing the Sugar Daddy with an experience. Where they feel they can trust you to an extent. You might say that at that point the marketing stops and the selling starts. All of your efforts are to get your Sugar Daddy to second base, and then from second to third. It's the selling process and finding about their needs, and third base is where a Sugar Daddy is interested in being in a relationship with you and they have made up their mind that they want to be with you, but you are not home yet because you have not set up a foundation to the relationship you want.

Depending on the connection with your potential Sugar Daddy, you can slide into home. Depending on where you are with this it can take a few days, weeks, or months depending on your target Sugar Daddy and his interest level. Then finally he responds the way you want. But it's really understanding how this Sugar Daddy game can transform your Sugar Daddy experience into a system of step-by-step things until ultimately you get home and in the Sugar Daddy relationship you are in. So that is your first area you have to master so that your Sugar Baby marketing is not random.

2. Sugar Baby Mindset

Number two is just as important. You might say that the Sugar Daddy game is the outer game and then there is the inner-game in which I call the Sugar Baby Mindset.

Certain things are easy for people and some things are hard. For example, one Sugar Baby might find it very easy to write her profile. But the same Sugar Baby may find it not only hard, but terrifying to ask for what she wants. And conversely, the person who finds it a breeze to ask for what she wants may freeze up when it comes to writing her profile.

What is easy for us is easy for us, and what is hard for us is hard for us. Period. You need to be perfectly ok about exactly where you are right now. After all, it's what you have to work with right now. We all have different starting points, but what counts is where you end up.

So, what issues do you have, what are your concerns, dilemmas, and where are you stuck at in your Sugar Baby marketing? For example, if you discover that the best approach to finding a Sugar Daddy is online vs offline, and you have issues writing your profile, then that is going to get in the way of attracting potential Sugar Daddies. You have to get past that old mindset on figuring out what to say out fear of not portraying yourself to capture the attention of a Sugar Daddy with your profile and stop blaming the dating site you are in if you aren't getting any results. You need to get to the other side and start to say what can I write to appeal to the Sugar Daddy I want. So what happens during the Sugar Baby marketing process is that we get stuck on some issue, fear, or concern or something we don't feel that we know well enough or fear of not finding a Sugar Daddy. Sugar Baby marketing mindset takes a central role because even if you know what to do and how to do it. If you are afraid, if you are stuck or uncertain nothing will happen. We have to surmount our old Sugar Baby mindset.

3. Sugar Baby Marketing Messages

Number three is the heart of Sugar Baby marketing. All Sugar Baby marketing is about *communication*. It is all about communicating to a potential Sugar Daddy is that you are the one for them. It's how your Sugar Daddy perceives you to be. I discovered that there are systems for that, and what I call that is Sugar Baby marketing syntax, and that is the order in how you present yourself to your Sugar Daddies to increase the chances of getting their attention and interest.

The first step of is getting their attention and that starts with your profile. Your profile consists of your picture, your headline, and the body of your personal ad. Each of the components of your personal ad plays a part including your engagement and interaction with potential Sugar Daddy when they respond to you. When you start to understand how each component works all of a sudden you have a process. You are providing your Sugar Daddy with an experience.

For example, a Sugar Baby was having issues attracting Sugar Daddies. Her issues were her approach on how she was coming across as she was attracting undesirable Sugar Daddies who just wanted sex and she was giving herself with nothing in return. She found herself stuck in a never-ending cycle. She reassessed her approach and now she is positioning herself more effectively to target her ideal Sugar Daddy without giving it up in hopes of receiving something from her potential. That basic marketing message is extraordinarily easy once you understand, but Sugar Babies don't do anything to change their approach and would rather get upset when things are not turning out in their favor.

4. Sugar Baby Marketing Materials

This simply consists of your profile and email correspondence. What you write. Your presentation of how you want to be perceived. The great thing about this is that there are processes, systems, structures that work much better than what the average Sugar Baby use to get better results through writing. Writing effectively increases your ability to connect with Sugar Daddies and now you are able to communicate with Sugar Daddies more clearly and put you in a better position to convey what is that you want to Sugar Daddies and guide them in the direction you want to take them in and that is getting you what you want.

5. The Sugar Baby Follow-Up

What holds this all together? If you don't do any form of following up with your potential Sugar Daddies after you engage with them you are at risk of losing their interest.

This is the area that some Sugar Babies avoid the most and obsess about. Whether they should wait until they hear back from their potential Sugar Daddy or worry about saying the wrong thing because of fear of rejection, but we have to master this and understand the system.

6. Sugar Baby Marketing Strategies

And number six is Sugar Baby marketing strategies. Here we have the most common strategies for Sugar Babies: The personal ad, Sugar Daddy engagement, responding to Sugar Daddy profiles, setting up a relationship, and asking for what we want all have a synergistic impact – its more than the sum of the parts. We pick our strategies and do them effectively. This is the way to put together your communication and a clear message but the strategy is the way you attract your potential Sugar Daddy. Ultimately you have to put all this together into a plan, as there are a lot of moving parts that you need to put together. I should have:

✓ A profile plan.

✓ Who am I targeting.

✓ Follow-up plan.

✓ How to ask for what I want plan.

✓ These are the actions I am going to take.

Being organized and being on top of things and having a structure is important, otherwise everything falls through the cracks.

7. Selling Yourself to Your Sugar Daddy

Selling yourself is included in the Sugar Baby lifestyle. Once you get to second base you have to know how to sell yourself to your potential Sugar Daddy. You need to have a methodology and a strategy. It's not just being on a Sugar Daddy dating site will find you a Sugar Daddy and you will get what you want just by communicating with a potential Sugar Daddy. You have to present yourself in a way that your potential Sugar Daddy would want to help you.

Here is the great thing – when you get better at all these parts you get more dates, and you can convert them into relationships strategically to get them to provide you what you want. You may connect with three potential Sugar Daddies, and out of those three you get one perfect Sugar Daddy. So just by improving your ability you can increase your results by 30% to 60% by just changing your approach and just by understanding everything in great detail in putting yourself in a better position with your target Sugar Daddy.

What you know and how you apply is directly connected to how successful you are with finding and attracting Sugar Daddies.

You might say you are great with finding Sugar Daddies but struggle with making a connection. But there are always ways you can improve and get better.

That's where you are. Now where do you want to go?

Your Sugar Baby Goals

What do you want out of this lifestyle?

So, what are your Sugar Baby goals? What I want you to do is think about it and be realistic of what you are looking for out of this lifestyle. Look if you don't do anything else do this: If you set your goals things can change dramatically because when you get clear on your Sugar Baby goals it sets a direction and creates context and increase motivation when we know what we want and have a clear picture on how we are going to get there.

What do you want out of this lifestyle? I wanted this lifestyle because I wanted to experience a different world than what I was accustomed to and find a Sugar Daddy to assist me within my lifestyle to achieve my personal goals.

Who are the kinds of Sugar Daddies you'd like to date ideally? Describe them and be clear. And one way to do this is to create a profile on your target Sugar Daddy and why him? Write down a description of your ideal

Sugar Daddy and fix that in your mind and get excited about it because it will shape your Sugar Baby marketing. It creates a direction of the foundation of what you set for this lifestyle. So many Sugar Babies will get into this lifestyle merely for the instant gratification that this lifestyle portrays and take any Sugar Daddy that shows interest in them and settling when they can have so much more.

What are you looking for from your Sugar Daddy? His financial generosity, mentorship, experiencing something new, traveling...Being clear of what you want out of this lifestyles will give you the lifestyle that you want. What is right for you will be different for every Sugar Baby.

For me, I wanted a Sugar Daddy who would compliment me on my business endeavors and starting a business was one of them. I combined my goals to attract the Sugar Daddy that would put me in reach to get me there faster which served as a guiding direction for me to achieve my goals instead of just randomly hoping that I find a Sugar Daddy who could just afford me. It is okay to share your goals with the exception of what you hope to gain financially with your potential Sugar Daddy to gauge their interest and capability in meeting your expectations.

This lifestyle isn't just about you. So, what are you willing do to get what you want? Are you willing to do what is necessary to live this lifestyle based on your potential

Sugar Daddy needs? I suggest you set your standards and know your value before your potential Sugar Daddy places one on you.

Are you willing to learn how to shift your thinking and beliefs in order to reach these goals?

Change Your Sugar Baby Mindset

So, the mindset that got you to where you are now is not the mindset to get you to where you want to go. You have to think outside the box, outside of your limitations.

For example asking for what you want is hard and you don't and allow your Sugar Daddy to guide the relationship as he sees it because you were afraid of how he might view you. You have to find ways to work on this mindset not only can I attract Sugar Daddies I can ask for what I want and get. And after a while you have cultivated this mindset it becomes easier because of your confidence. You have to always be willing to move on because otherwise you will trap yourself in a fear of losing your Sugar Daddy and that is the surest way to lose a Sugar Daddy.

What's between where you are and your goals?

You want to bridge the gap to connect all the pieces together. Here you are at one point and there is your goal

251

at another. You have to understand what is in between that gap to get to the goal. You can't just strap a rocket packet to your back and fly over to your goal.

What is your gap? What issues, challenges that separates you from getting what you want out of this lifestyle? You have to understand what they are so you can meet it realistically.

The 5 Big Challenges of Sugar Baby Marketing Success

1. Lack of direction and Commitment. If we are in that place it is hard to make a step because we don't know where we are going and lack of clarity.

2. Insufficient knowledge and skills. We don't understand the processes and techniques to get good results consistently as it will take more work.

3. Lack of systems. How can you get to where you are when you don't know what stage of the game you are in and it brings your energy down? Take a step back and reassess why you want this lifestyle.

4. Unfavorable circumstances. For example; living at home with parents, don't have a job, don't have a car, don't have the funds to sign up to a dating site. What is your situation? Are you in a relationship...as that is a circumstance that can be problematic for you and it's

not going to be easy. You want to be in the best possible conditions but things don't have to be perfect for you to take the next step. This is broad and somewhat general so there are a lot of different circumstances externally that we have to deal with and we can't make them disappear automatically.

5. Bad Sugar Baby mindset. If you have a bad mindset in general and you don't feel that you can do a certain thing or you must have a certain look. All of these can stop you cold if you don't face. I can't tell you how much I worked on my mindset. I bought books on Sugar Daddy dating, and I did a lot of that stuff because if I was stuck in a bad mindset I wouldn't move forward and with that I can learn whatever I need to learn with a great attitude to find a way. We want to get to this place.

Developing a great Sugar Baby Mindset takes time, effort, and in some instances a willingness to make changes.

I received an Email from a Sugar Baby that said: "I'm going through your blog and reading the articles trying to revamp my profile but I am getting confused because I just don't know what to say. Please Help!"

We cannot approach Sugar Baby marketing from the old self that resists Sugar Baby marketing. We won't find time for it, or we'll find ways to creatively avoid it. The Sugar Baby Mindset is the most important part of our work.

How does your Sugar Baby Mindset impact your Sugar Baby Marketing?

It impacts it totally.

If you don't take your Sugar Baby Mindset into account it will undermine and sabotage your Sugar Baby Marketing Plans. But only every time.

So let's work on three of the most important Sugar Baby marketing principles and activities - Marketing your Message to potential Sugar Daddies, Sugar Baby Marketing Strategies, and the Selling Process to your Sugar Daddy- and integrate your Sugar Baby Mindset into them.

Marketing Messages

Your Marketing Messages, both verbal and written, are the foundation of your Sugar Baby marketing. Since marketing is 100% communication, if you're not communicating clearly about the value of what you have to offer, you weaken everything else in your Sugar Baby marketing.

There's nothing overly complicated here. You simply answer this question: Why Should a Sugar Daddy date you?

If you can answer that question clearly, you can get the attention and interest of just about any potential Sugar Daddy.

You can expand on that answer through your profile (strategically), email correspondence when engaging with potential SD's, but at their core they all communicate the same thing: "Why a Sugar Daddy should date you?" That establishes your Sugar Baby Allure!

But in practice, this can be challenging, not because the formula is complicated, but because of mindset issues. Simply put, our limited thinking and beliefs get in the way:

I don't know how to setup a relationship.

What if they perceive me to be an escort or gold-digger?

I just can't find the right words.

What if they don't want to date my race?

What if I am too old?

Then we put more focus on these thoughts and beliefs than our Sugar Baby marketing message and find ourselves caught in confusion, doubt, worry, uncertainty and lack of confidence.

And your Sugar Baby marketing efforts go down the drain.

The solution is not to try harder but to question those thoughts and beliefs. You need to undermine them by asking if they are true, what it's costing you to think them and literally strip them bare for the nonsense they really are.

More on working on your Sugar Baby mindset in the next two sections:

Sugar Baby Marketing Strategies

Once you have a marketing message, you need a vehicle or vehicles for these messages. Profile, Communicating with potential Sugar Daddies via the telephone/text messages, email follow ups, Contacting a Sugar Daddy first, etc.

None of these are particularly difficult; they are all step-by-step processes. They are something you can learn with a little study and patience by starting small and working towards bigger things, such as mastering your Sugar Baby profile.

But guess what? Implementing these marketing activities are often hijacked, not by circumstances or lack of time, but by the same kind of constrictive thinking and beliefs. We often defeat ourselves before we start.

I can't find the right words.

I don't know what to say what it is that I want.

Should I be specific in my profile?

These potential Sugar Daddies only want to date a blonde.

I am unsure about asking for an allowance.

I promise you that effective Sugar Baby marketing will be impossible if you cloud your mind with this kind of thinking.

I was helping a Sugar Baby with her profile. She was off to a good start but it needed more work. I provided her with suggestions on what areas she could improve and I also provided examples to help illustrate my point and reasoning behind why I would use a certain word.

A few months passed by and she reached out to me frustrated then when I had helped her before. She confessed and informed me she used the exact copy of the profile that was found in my eBook. She was wondering why she wasn't getting the results she was seeking.

I wasn't disappointed that she used the exact copy. I was actually sad that she wasted time that she could not get back. She could have been in a different situation than where she was. I explained that I had a specific target that I was attracting and quality is far better than quantity. Plus, I used the profile on a different medium than a Sugar Daddy dating site (which makes a difference on how it was used and to whom I was targeting.)

When we explored why she didn't take the suggestions and commits that I had given her, it became clear that she had got caught up into those old beliefs again, and didn't try to revamp her profile despite the absolute evidence that her profile was lacking. She just didn't want to try and wanted something of a quick fix to try to get results and months later she was right where she started.

Once you've really questioned your limiting beliefs, and revealed them for what they really are: ploys to avoid writing, or not asking for what you want...you need to look in the other direction:

If it was impossible to believe those thoughts anymore, who would you be and what would you do? Isn't it obvious that you'd move into action with less fear and hesitation?

Your Selling Process to Your Sugar Daddy

This is one of your most high-leverage Sugar Baby marketing activities ever. If you've used your Sugar Baby marketing messages while implementing your marketing activities, ultimately you'll connect with qualified potential Sugar Daddies.

When you connect with a potential Sugar Daddy you have to sell yourself in order for them to do what you want.

When you are trying to set up a relationship it consists of five main parts. The first four are understanding the psychology of Sugar Daddies, what they say they want, what they really want, and what they'll contribute.

Then the fifth part is telling your potential Sugar Daddy how you can be the person who can fulfill their needs (the value of what you bring into the relationship). Oh yes, and in order to make it this far they have to like you!

Sounds simple, and it is, however, there are many subtle skills to selling yourself to your potential Sugar Daddy and it takes time to study and practice them. If you do, you'll find your success rate goes way up.

But of course, your old Mindset can be just as destructive here as anywhere else in the Sugar Baby marketing process. Here are a few limiting thoughts and beliefs you may be familiar with:

They won't want to date me.

I don't want to be pushy.

I feel too awkward for asking for what I want.

Seeing a pattern here? All of these limiting thoughts and beliefs have a similar tone and taste. They are fear-based. They are about avoidance of any possibility of rejection. And if you believe them, they stop you cold.

If you are ever going to be successful at Sugar Daddy Dating, you can't just learn the basic strategies and tactics otherwise you will end up with the rest of the horde of SB's vying for the same SD you are targeting. You'll keep bumping into these limiting thoughts and beliefs without even realizing it and then make up reasons why Sugar Daddy dating isn't going your way and start blaming the dating site that you on and find yourself jumping from different sites and not getting any results and out this lifestyle altogether.

Instead, you need to take your Sugar Baby Mindset into account and confront them directly. Before long you'll discover: They aren't really true, believing them is costing you a lot, their payoff is staying in your comfort zone, and if you are willing to look at what might be possible without attachments to these beliefs, you'll discover a world that was invisible to you before.

Sugar Baby
Case Studies

There's no better way to teach than by telling a story. Here are two women with dilemmas who reached out to me, and you can read and think about their issues and consider my advice to them and the lessons learned.

Case Study #1

Misplaced Sugar Baby: I'm simply interested in some tips on how to keep the sd/sb relationship strong long term despite a fifteen-year difference in our ages. I'm in my late thirties and he's in his late fifties and we are really into each other, but is emotionally unavailable at times which he apologizes for but it gives me mixed signals. What is going on in that almost sixty-year-old head of his. What do men that age expect?

Taylor: Before I jump into what you are asking. Let me ask you a question: What is it that you want from him? Really want?

Misplaced Sugar Baby: I want to know how relevant I am to him.

Taylor: When you are wanting more from the relationship then what the other is displaying it is downright nerve-wracking and frustrating.

As women we tend to think with our feelings and we have to know where we are within a relationship regardless of how the relationship is going and in the meantime the man is perfectly just fine with how things are and they shy away with labels or even expressing themselves.

Older men display their actions with how they treat you and what they are doing for you which reflect how relevant you are. I always take on the mindset that every time that I am around the person that I am with, the relationship renews itself. This allows me to stay upbeat and keeps the relationship fresh. I am constantly on the lookout for doing something different or if I do the same thing I make something about it different to experience something new which keeps me interesting and that sustains the relationship. If I don't go this route the relationship will hit a plateau.

So how relevant are you keeping yourself with the relationship?

Misplaced Sugar Baby: Thank you so much for the insight and your questions; you really hit the nail on the head regarding my situation. When I see him, things are really good, we laugh, he asks me what I want to do, wants me to be happy and we have a great intimate relationship. My issues probably stem from the physical distance between us. A two-hour flight or five-hour drive gets tiring fast.

Our relationship is new, only a few months in and I am realizing that, as you said, I have been putting more emotional worry in areas where it isn't necessary. Being older, and male (smile) he simply doesn't seem to need as much emotionally from me to be comfortable with our relationship. So, I've been curbing it and that had helped. He has told me that I am his focus. Fantastic, right? I think that I worry that that might change if I don't inform him more how much he means to me. I have a hard time simply believing that it "just is" and that he fine. I am really confident, especially in relationships but knowing that I need his income right now, is throwing off my balance which bugs the hell out of me.

He is my first SD, my allowance is three thousand per month, to start out and I see him about once a month. Staying relevant is the key, that is exactly what I think too! It is so hard to do via text, I fear that plateau creeping up on me so I send pictures, sext him, I'd talk to him more about work but that never seemed to I interest him. This is where I need help. (Our schedules are opposing, so talking on the phone is tough.) I'm trying to find more common interests before his is bored to death!

Luckily, he is flying me out to see him in next week (he bought the tickets) but man do I feel boring, as the younger person in the relationship. It's on me to keep the fire burning, but he's not replying to the pics immediately like he used to (uh oh) he says they are great, any suggestions on my next step? I usually confidently have a man on board displaying his affections first and regularly, is this just how most Sugar Daddies are?

Oh, he just ended a five-year relationship with a SB that he really liked but she strung him along for the last year so he said no more and picked me to focus on. No pressure right? So maybe he needs less, not more to really want me more, this only adds to my confusion. I don't want to overdo what he may feel is already really good but the fear of that plateau, is pushing me to possibly overdo it and ruin it anyway. Bottom line: I want to stay relevant, are my concerns mucking it up?

Taylor: Well you are letting your relevancy get the best of you. You should focus on enjoying the relationship and getting to know him better and making each time together that much enjoyable. For example what kinds of things interest him? Do they interest you too? Perhaps you can find something to do that he would like and you too together. I have a Sugar Daddy that was into music and I purchased tickets to a show for both of us to go to and he was thrilled. Unexpected. *(Not saying* *that I played this card a lot but every once in a while I will do something special in a big way that is cost effective).*

You asked if all Sugar Daddies are like this. No, not all Sugar Daddies are like that. It truly depends on the type of Sugar Daddy and his personality. I had a Sugar Daddy who loved doing things for me and planning trips all the time and going to shows, festivals, and road-trips out the blue and dinning adventures. And I had a Sugar Daddy who worked a lot and I would take on the role of finding things for us to do. So it truly depends on his type. I will have to work on a list of things a Sugar Baby can do to keep the relationship interesting (maybe like a top 50)...I will have to keep you posted on that one.

Misplaced Sugar Baby: Here's my final question regarding this issue. In your experience, is it better to have one SD at a time or to juggle a few just in case the well runs dry with one, you have another as backup. And if yes to the latter, should they be selected from separate websites so that the actual SD's think that you are exclusive?

Taylor: It truly depends on you! And what it is that you are wanting out of this lifestyle and where you want it to take you. Do you want to be with more than one? Why have many when you can seek-out someone that can afford you vs. have two or three. Plus you don't want to lose yourself in this lifestyle either. I prefer to build long-lasting relationships and in the process find additional streams of income by using the generosity of my Sugar Daddy to put myself in a different income bracket. There are girls out there that Sugar Daddy date and make this their only form of income, but what happens is that they turn into escorts.

Misplaced Sugar Baby: Thank you so much, Taylor. You have helped me turn around my situation and I am already seen the results! You taught me that balance is key. Your advice to keep it honest has helped me regain my focus in this relationship!

Case Study #2

Allowance Seeking Sugar Baby: I've done my research (read your blog like it was the bible) and I am discussing allowance with a potential SD right now. My research has told me to wait to discuss an arrangement in person however, I rather not waste time if what he can provide is significantly below what I am expecting. He makes $100-175K a year. I expect an allowance of $2,000 (he has already made it clear that gift/ travel will not be deducted from my allowance). The issue is that he has asked me how much I want. I am not sure if I should just flat out say $2,000 (it is a little more than 10% of what he will be bringing home a month) or if I should request that he tells me how much he is comfortable dedicating to an arrangement.

I apologize if this sounds redundant of self explanatory but I this is my first negotiation and I want to ensure that my expectations are realistic.

Taylor: Just like you have an expectation of an allowance of $2,000, men ask us how much we want to see if they can afford us. It works both ways. So the question isn't if he can afford you but if he wants to spend his money on you. So how you come across and how he perceives you to be matters. You can ask him ideally how much of a contribution he is looking to provide to get a better understanding of what he is thinking to know your next move.

Allowance Seeking Sugar Baby: Thank you for your insight and advice. Here's what happened: I told him (in very sugar-coated way) of my expectations of $2,000 a month. He answered that it was well out of his budget. Out of curiosity I asked him what the parameters of his budget totaled. To be honest, I am not sure if he was offended or disappointed. He told me, "Do not negotiate price in this type relationship. Decide how much support you truly need for your goals, and stay with it. Negotiating 'how much' puts you into a different category of woman where I am sure you don't belong."

To be honest, I am not sure of what he meant by that (was he referring to me as an escort?) but I feel like he didn't want me to settle. Needless to say, an arrangement will not be established. However, got more out of our emails back and forth than any amount of money. I received knowledge, experience and confidence.

If a potential SD can tell me not to settle, to state my expectations, and stand my ground, than I have every bit of a right to expect that much from myself. I also take it as a learning experience and I will ask a potential of their expectations of a monthly stipend before I say what I expect. Anyways, I just wanted to tell you thank you!

Taylor: You learned what a lot of Sugar Babies will never get. I get hundreds of questions and majority asks me "Taylor, What's those magic words I can say to get what I want?"... And they fail to realize that there is a process to influencing a Sugar Daddy.

You have to change their perception because you are already being viewed less by being a Sugar Baby. Your actions complete your story. Sugar Babies are in a hurry to get what they want and feel as though they should be direct and up front because they do not want to waste their time. And as a result they come across as escorts, self-absorbed needy woman when the relationship being formed is mutual.

It's hard to put our own egos aside but if you can manage that you would be a better position to understanding what a Sugar Daddy is looking for even without having them say it. You see a real Sugar Daddy who can afford you if their budget allows is not going to give you anything unless her likes you and trusts you.

Conclusion

Thank you for reading *The Sugar Daddy Formula*. This book has given you a practical, step-by-step formula to find a Sugar Daddy, bring him into your life, and keep him interested. You have everything you need to get started immediately, and I really hope that you actually apply what you've learned here. We've covered a lot of ground and now you have the knowledge and insight you need to enter the exciting world of Sugar Babies and find the Sugar Daddy of your dreams!

Before I end the book, I'm going to skip the hand-wavy niceties and dish out some tough love. Ready? Listen up!

Sugar Babies beware. Don't be naive about the ulterior motives of the men you find. They will come across as being wealthy when they are not, and they want you to prove yourself to them by having sex with them before anything is established. These Sugar Daddy dating websites set them up with a straight-shot to have sex with you, and when they do they are gone and on to the next one.

Why should a Sugar Daddy invest in you when you're easy? That's why most Sugar Daddy sites are FREE for women. With so many women on these sites they can have their cake and sleep with you too. Don't sleep with men in hopes of getting something out of it before a relationship has been established.

Be careful! A proper Sugar Daddy isn't going to pressure you for sex.

So, aspiring Sugar Baby, don't put out on the first date, and always verify your potential Sugar Daddy to make sure he is what he say he is and also proving himself to you too.

I want you to think about what will happen if you do *not* apply what you have learned in this book, and if you continue to live the life that you're living, dating the same types of guys you've been dating, and feeling resentful that you aren't doing what you really want to be doing.

Now think about what your life will be like if you apply what you have learned in this book. Think about the men you'll meet, the lifestyle you'll live, and how happy you'll feel. As you've learned in this book, that is totally possible for you – all you need to do is actually go out there and do it.

Being a Sugar Baby isn't easy. This lifestyle is a journey with both pitfalls and rewards. The world can be unkind, cruel, and full of hate. It's my hope that, using the tools and information in this book, you will get closer to the lifestyle that you want to live. I want you to experience the amazing Sugar Baby lifestyle that you desire and deserve.

Don't make your Sugar Daddy solely responsible for your happiness. Be realistic in your expectations. You have a tremendous influence on the quality and fate of your relationship. You really do. If you know the game, the rewards you will reap will be limitless.

I wish you success in finding newly discovered treasures within yourself and happiness on your journey.

Sugar Baby Resources:
Information that You can Use to Help Increase Your Success with Sugar Daddies

*I*f you're interested in understanding Sugar Daddy dating, making better Sugar Baby choices and decisions, and setting yourself up with the information you need to cut your learning curve in half.

There's a game being played around you, and if you do what everyone else does, you've already lost. If what you are doing isn't getting the results you are seeking. Change the direction but not the goal of why you want this lifestyle.

Join a Community of Sugar Babies that will Support You in Your Lifestyle

Are you navigating this lifestyle alone? (Worse, did you have someone who sabotaged you? Maybe they said, "No man will give you what you want. You are just and es-cort." "You are not Sugar Baby material?" "You are too old to be a Sugar Baby?") *Ugh.* Now think of another time you SUCCEEDED—where you actually did better than you thought you could have. Did you have a friend encouraging you? Were you part of a group that supported you? Connect with others who are here to help each other with personal issues that we encounter. It's a 'private' group and you must request to join.

Send me a private confidential email and request the information: sbsupport@sugardaddyformula.com

SugaInsider Sweet Talk LIVE Radio (Listen to Sugar Babies Openly Share Their Secrets and Strategies)

I'm here to tell you after having a Sugar Daddy provide me with $100,000.00, coaching Sugar Babies 1-on-1, helping thousands of Sugar Babies get the results they want that there is always a SMART way and a HARD way to achieve Sugar Baby success. Knowing the difference is a RARE and valuable skill to have. And that's what I will be sharing with you on the SugaInsider Sweet Talk LIVE Radio.

http://thesugardaddyformula.com/
sugar-daddy-podcast-sugainsider-sweet-talk

Sugar Baby eCourse: FIND, ATTRACT Your Ideal Sugar Daddy AND Get What You Want

If you want a detailed guide and handholding to Sugar Daddy Dating, crafting your Sugar Baby profile, finding the right site for you, guides and examples of how to package and present yourself, how to position what you want (and strategies to sidestep them), please check out my Sugar Baby eCourse.

https://thesugardaddyformula.com/sugar-baby-ecourse/

Invest in Your Lifestyle and I Will Personally Help You Get What You WANT!

If you don't want to leave anything to chance, my Sugar Baby coaching services are for you. I'll help you see what you can't see, and overcome the things you can see (but don't know how to fix). There's a big difference between knowing what to do and actually DOING it. My Private Coaching and Sugar Baby Mastermind programs are for the Sugar Babies who want RESULTS. I'll help assist you with finding a Sugar Baby Action Plan with YOU.

http://thesugardaddyformula.com/
complimentary-sugar-baby-strategy-session/

Sugar Profile Writing Services

Your online dating profile is the gateway to making Sugar Daddy Dating online work. And whether you don't have the time to write one, you can't find the right words, or you don't like writing our Sugar Profile Writers will build the kind of Sugar Baby Profile that sets the foundation for your Sugar Baby success.

http://thesugardaddyformula.com/sugar-profile-writer/

Your Personal GPS through Complicated Sugar Daddy Dating Obstacles (Online Sugar Baby Resource Book)

We all feel some sort of way about asking for what we want. The key is knowing what triggers your Sugar Daddy, how you position yourself to ask for what you want, the timing of it, and of course the RIGHT Man who can afford you. Don't leave anything to chance. Finding a Sugar Daddy isn't luck, it's a decision.

https://thesugardaddyformula.com/resources/

Let's Talk!

I'd love to hear from you! Share your Sugar Baby experiences… your triumphs and heartbreaks, and your successes and disappointments. I invite you to contact me and I'll send you free information about the services that I offer that can help you find the Sugar Daddy of your dreams.

http://thesugardaddyformula.com

I look forward to hearing from you!

Taylor

Made in the USA
Las Vegas, NV
28 February 2024